Holier than Thou

Saudi Arabia's Islamic Opposition

Joshua Teitelbaum

Policy Papers no. 52

THE WASHINGTON INSTITUTE FOR NEAR EAST POLICY

© 2000 by the Washington Institute for Near East Policy

Second Printing

Published in 2000 in the United States of America by the Washington Institute for Near East Policy, 1828 L Street NW, Suite 1050, Washington, DC 20036.

Library of Congress Cataloging-in-Publication Data

Teitelbaum, Joshua
    Holier than thou : Saudi Arabia's Islamic opposition / Joshua Teitelbaum
        p. cm. — (Policy papers ; no. 52)
    Includes bibliographical references.
    ISBN 0-944029-35-3 (pbk)
    1. Saudi Arabia—Politics and government—20th century. 2. Islam and politics—Saudi Arabia.
3. Opposition (Political science)—Saudi Arabia.
4. Political violence—Saudi Arabia. I. Title. II. Policy papers (Washington Institute for Near East Policy); no. 52.
DS244.63 .T45 1999
320.9538'09'049—dc21   99-055430
                                    CIP

Cover photo © Corbis/Bettman.
Cover design by Monica Neal Hertzman.

The Author

J oshua Teitelbaum is a research fellow at the Moshe Dayan Center for Middle Eastern and African Studies and instructor in the Overseas Students Program at Tel Aviv University. His fields of specialization include the history of the Arabian Peninsula, specifically Saudi Arabia, and Palestinian history and politics. He is the author of *The Rise and Fall of the Hashemite Kingdom of Arabia* (New York and London, forthcoming in 2001).

Dr. Teitelbaum received his Ph.D. in the field of Modern Middle Eastern History from Tel Aviv University in 1996. In 1997, while he was The Washington Institute's Meyerhoff Fellow, he began research for this Policy Paper.

• • •

Table of Contents

For Jacqueline

Psalms 69:14

Acknowledgments

This study was researched while I was the Meyerhoff Visiting Fellow at The Washington Institute for Near East Policy. Thanks to the Institute's director, Robert Satloff, for his hospitality and for arranging meetings. The Institute's director for research, Patrick Clawson, read the manuscript diligently and made many constructive comments. I would also like to thank the research assistants and interns of the Institute for valiantly tracking down source material. David Elias in Tel Aviv deserves a special note of thanks for devoting his expertise and time above and beyond the call of duty in helping to research this study. Emily Cooper's research assistance was also of great value. My Dayan Center colleagues, Joseph Kostiner and Meir Litvak, as always, have been wonderful intellectual companions as this study took shape. Thanks also to Dayan Center fellows Paul Rivlin and Onn Winckler for their help with the statistics, and to Aryeh Ezra, Haim Gal, Marion Gliksberg, and Dorit Paret of the Dayan Center Library and Press Archive. Monica Hertzman of The Washington Institute has been a wonderful editor. I am indebted to them all for their contributions, but responsibility for the points made in this paper remains with me.

This book is dedicated to my wife and friend Jacqueline, a source of strength and support.

Joshua Teitelbaum
Tel Aviv
October 2000

Preface

There are few countries governed more closely by the strictures of Islam than the Kingdom of Saudi Arabia. Ironically, as historian Joshua Teitelbaum points out in this fascinating Policy Paper, radical fundamentalists still pose the most substantial security threat to the ruling Al Sa'ud family, guardians of Islam's two holiest shrines and the world's largest source of oil.

Composed of both mainstream Sunni and minority Shi'i radicals, Saudi Arabia's Islamic opposition poses a new and original threat to the Al Sa'ud by questioning the legitimacy of the family's longstanding claim to govern according to Islamic *shari'a* law. Indeed, the radical fundamentalists stand poised to shake the public image of Saudi Arabia as the only Islamic country to have achieved a successful marriage between tradition and modernity.

This is not just some ideological challenge to the Saudi system of government. On the contrary, the Islamic opposition poses a real and present danger to the Saudi regime and to U.S. forces that provide a security umbrella to the Saudis and other Gulf countries. Radical Islamists in Saudi Arabia have already left their violent mark in such bloody attacks as the 1996 al-Khobar Towers bombing against U.S. forces in Dharan and in the ongoing campaigns of the notorious Usama bin Ladin, whose arrest remains a top priority for both U.S. and Saudi law enforcement officials. Indeed, the common interest shared by America and Saudi Arabia in containing a form of religious extremism that targets both countries equally is one of the cornerstones of U.S–Saudi relations in the first decade of the twenty-first century.

In this, the second Washington Institute Policy Paper of 2000 to focus on the Saudi kingdom, Dr. Teitelbaum presents an incisive and comprehensive survey of Saudi Arabia's Islamic opposition. Based on his years of expertise in Saudi religion, society, and politics, as well as specialization in the history of the Arabian Peninsula, Dr. Teitelbaum—a former Meyerhoff Fellow at the Institute—provides clear answers to the fundamental questions about this radical challenge to regional stability: Who are the Islamists? What are their goals? How serious is the threat? What can be done to combat it?

Despite sharp differences with the United States on critical policy questions, especially the Arab–Israeli peace process, Saudi Arabia remains one of the most strategically vital countries in perhaps the world's most volatile region. Understanding the threats it faces can only improve America's ability to preserve and protect U.S. interests in this critical area. To advance that goal, The Washington Institute is proud to present this important research.

Michael Stein
Chairman

Fred S. Lafer
President

Executive Summary

Although Saudi Arabia is popularly perceived as the most religious of Arab countries, the question of who in the kingdom determines its dominant Islamic discourse has been the subject of controversy since the state's founding. The formation of Saudi Arabia in the early twentieth century involved the unique harnessing of the Wahhabi *da'wa* (creed) in the service of the political aims of the Al Sa'ud, the Saudi family. The regime has not been without its detractors, but for the most part the Al Sa'ud has been able to coopt or repress them. Since the Gulf War, however, the social and economic problems that have plagued the country have led to the rise of a radical Islamic fundamentalist movement that has challenged Saudi Arabia's public persona as the one Islamic country that has successfully combined tradition and modernity.

Radical Islamic Fundamentalism in Saudi Arabia

A common term for modern political Islamic ideology is Islamic fundamentalism. In the Saudi case, however, it is official Islam that is fundamentalist, in that the country claims to be governed by the fundamentals of Islamic law. The subject of this study, the antiestablishment Islamic movement in Saudi Arabia, is therefore best described as a radical fundamentalist movement.

Unlike most Sunni radical fundamentalist leaders, the leaders of Saudi Arabia's movement are not laymen but rather *'ulama* (clerics) who have rebelled against the very fundamentalist system that created them. The movement—an agglomeration of groups with no acknowledged leader—got its start in the 1950s and 1960s, but for several reasons it grew in strength in the 1980s and 1990s. One factor has been the rise of a new generation of young leaders educated in Saudi

Islamic universities. Another is the decline in oil prices, which led Saudi Arabia to cut many of its subsidies and social programs for its citizens. A final factor is a growing resentment at the presence of U.S. troops in Saudi Arabia and the Persian Gulf region.

To quell dissatisfaction over the years, the Saudi regime has regularly attempted to coopt or marginalize the establishment 'ulama. At various times in Saudi history, groups of 'ulama—usually from the outer circles of the establishment—have challenged the Al Sa'ud. The first such occurrence was the Ikhwan rebellion in 1927–1930, which ended with the country's founder, Ibn Sa'ud, coopting the leading 'ulama into the nascent, modern state system, as part of a policy that one scholar has termed "encapsulation." As the Saudi state became more bureaucratized, incorporation of the 'ulama into the state administration diminished their role.

Faysal's Order

Faysal bin 'Abd al-'Aziz, Saudi Arabia's third king, developed the current modus vivendi between the 'ulama and the state, part of a multifaceted system governing state–society relations termed "Faysal's order." During his reign and afterward, several quasi-judicial bodies were established ostensibly to supplement the *shari'a* (Islamic law), but they actually restricted it. Faysal established the *majlis hay'at kibar al-'ulama* (the Council of Senior 'Ulama) in 1971 with the country's top *'alim* (Islamic scholar), 'Abd al-'Aziz Bin Baz, as its leader.

Not all were pleased by Faysal's order, however. The greatest opposition the regime faced occurred on November 20, 1979, which corresponded to 1 Muharram 1400, the first day of the new Islamic century. On that day, two oppositionists, Juhayman bin Muhammad al-'Utaybi and Muhammad bin 'Abdallah al-Qahtani, organized several hundred followers in attacking the Grand Mosque—the holiest site in Islam—an event one commentator called "the Return of the Ikhwan." The Saudi regime turned to the establishment 'ulama to issue a *fatwa* (edict) against al-'Utaybi's group and sanction their removal by force from the Meccan Haram. A fatwa was in fact issued, but although the establishment 'ulama were aware of al-'Utaybi's opposition activities prior to the attack, the fatwa was not an outright condemnation. It was clear then that the establishment 'ulama and the opposition were not totally at odds.

Loss of Control: Islamic Opposition in the Wake of the Gulf War

A decade later, the Iraqi invasion of Kuwait and the subsequent Gulf War again emboldened radical Sunni fundamentalists. At the request of the Saudi regime, the Council of Senior 'Ulama issued a fatwa permitting the arrival of non-Muslim troops in Saudi Arabia during Operations Desert Shield and Desert Storm. Yet, this fatwa was rather grudging in tone, again demonstrating the increased degree of common ground between the establishment 'ulama and the radicals.

For many radical Sunni fundamentalist shaykhs, the fatwa crossed a red line; part of the regime's social contract with its subjects involved its protecting them, but clearly it was not militarily able to do so. Two relatively young 'ulama, Shaykh Salman bin Fahd al-'Awda and Shaykh Safar bin 'Abd al-Rahman al-Hawali, who have become known as the "Awakening Shaykhs," led the radical Sunni fundamentalist movement after the Iraqi invasion. Through the distribution of audiotaped lectures, their popularity reached its peak with the Gulf crisis and, according to sympathetic sources, was given further impetus by "the arrival of American troops in the *bilad al-haramayn* [land of the two holy shrines, Mecca and Medina]."

King Fahd's announcement in early November 1990 that he planned to initiate political reforms, including the creation of a *majlis al-shura* (consultative council), led radical Sunni fundamentalists to issue the "Letter of Demands" in May 1991. This document represented the first organized attempt by not only the radical 'ulama but also some establishment 'ulama to increase the power of religious figures in political decision making and to reject the increased marginalization of the 'ulama. The regime succeeded in putting down this opposition by arresting some of its members and removing others from office, but support for the agenda of the radical 'ulama did not diminish.

In the summer of 1992, the King Sa'ud University Committee for Reform and Advice organized the writing of a detailed memorandum of grievances and submitted it to Bin Baz. Al-Hawali, al-'Awda, 'Abdallah bin al-Jibrin, and 'Abdallah al-Jalali wrote the introduction to the memorandum, which sought both to remove the government and its official 'ulama from their role as the sole arbiters of Islam in the state and to return religion to the more decentralized nature it enjoyed before Ibn Sa'ud and before Faysal inaugurated his reforms. King Fahd fought back, enlisting the Council of Senior 'Ulama to counter the memorandum. Yet, again, the response of the establishment 'ulama showed the increasing sympathy for the radicals, as seven of the council members abstained from the proceedings.

The Founding of the CDLR

In May 1993, six radical fundamentalists publicly declared the establishment of the Committee for the Defense of Legitimate Rights (CDLR), which portrayed itself as a human rights organization in an effort to garner support in the West. Saudi authorities were quick to crush the CDLR; the group's spokesman, Muhammad al-Mas'ari, was forced into exile in London, where he established the CDLR headquarters in April 1994.

The organization concentrated on what it saw as the corruption and favoritism of the Saudi royal family at the expense of the public purse. The CDLR's public image was that of a sophisticated, enlightened group encouraging debate in the kingdom. It attacked the very foundation of the Saudi system by calling into question the age-old alliance between the 'ulama and the *umara* (princes).

When the regime arrested the Awakening Shaykhs in September 1994, the CDLR viciously lashed out. Although not directly endorsing violence and sometimes actually disavowing it, the CDLR warned that violence might result if the regime continued to oppress opposition activists. Meanwhile, it tried to fill the void following the arrests. In 1995, it became more strident in its attacks on the *'ulama al-sulta* (regime's scholars) who legitimized the royal family's activities.

In 1996, however, the organization experienced an acrimonious rupture because of al-Mas'ari's participation in two fanatical groups: *Hizb al-Tahrir* (the Liberation Party) and a breakaway faction, *al-Muhajirun* (the Emigrés). The CDLR deteriorated during 1996, and al-Mas'ari declared bankruptcy in January 1997; many of his former backers had shifted support to the CDLR's former London representative, Sa'd al-Faqih, who founded the Movement for Islamic Reform in Arabia (MIRA). In the meantime, MIRA developed into an organization that presented a more reasonable image than al-Mas'ari's CDLR. Currently, MIRA remains the only organized voice of the radical fundamentalist opposition in Saudi Arabia. Nevertheless, the overseas Saudi opposition lost much of its momentum after the split in the CDLR.

The Saudi 'Afghans' Strike

The Awakening Shaykhs and groups such as CDLR and MIRA essentially espoused nonviolence to change the government through vocal opposition. Not all groups chose the path of relative nonviolence, however, particularly the Saudi veterans of the war against the Soviet Union in Afghanistan.

In November 1995, the U.S. mission to the Saudi Arabian National Guard was bombed; it was then the largest attack of its kind in Saudi history, and three previously unknown groups claimed responsibility. The first break in the investigation occurred in early February 1996, when Pakistan announced it had deported Hasan al-Surayhi, a Saudi citizen who had been a *mujahid* (holy warrior) in Afghanistan, to Saudi Arabia. Al-Surayhi was never seen again, but he may have provided essential information to the Saudis.

Indeed, the regime later arrested and subsequently executed four men for the bombing, three of whom were veterans of the Afghan fighting. The men had been influenced by Usama bin Ladin, who represented the "jihadist" wing of the Saudi opposition. Bin Ladin criticized the Saudi regime and called for the expulsion of U.S. troops from Saudi Arabia. In April 1994, the regime announced that it was stripping Bin Ladin of his Saudi citizenship.

Bin Ladin stopped short of calling for violent attacks on the Saudi regime but harshly criticized it for imprisoning "our 'ulama"—a reference to al-'Awda and al-Hawali. In mid-February 1998, the London newspaper *al-Quds al-'Arabi* published Bin Ladin's "Declaration of the World Islamic Front for Jihad against the Jews and the Crusaders," and Bin Ladin also issued a fatwa stating that it is every Muslim's duty to kill Americans and their allies. The U.S. holds Bin Ladin responsible for the August 1998 bombing of the American embassies in Tanzania and Kenya. Not surprisingly, apprehending Bin Ladin is a priority for both the United States and Saudi Arabia.

The Shi'i Opposition and the Bombing of the U.S. Barracks in Dhahran

Saudi Arabia's minority Shi'i population has never been a threat to the regime, but there were violent indigenous disturbances in 1979 and 1980, known to Shi'i activists as the *intifada* (uprising) of the Eastern Province, and Iranian-sponsored terrorism as well in that economically and politically deprived region. Much of the Saudi Shi'i opposition was broken and in exile during the Persian Gulf War, although its members had founded an organization in the 1980s, the *Munazzamat al-Thawra al-Islamiyya* (Organization of the Islamic Revolution). To refashion its image, the organization changed its name to *al-Haraka al-Islahiyya* (the Reform Movement), and in 1991 it began to publish *al-Jazira al-'Arabiyya* in London and Arabian Monitor in Washington.

The June 1996 bombing of the al-Khobar Towers in Dhahran, however, was thought to be the work of Saudi Shi'is. Three groups claimed credit for the attack, but many believed that Iran was somehow involved. The Saudis began to clamp down on their Shi'i minority, and in early September, Shi'i activists in Saudi Arabia went public with accusations that Saudi authorities were arresting their compatriots.

In January 1997, U.S. sources, reportedly relying on information given to them by the head of Saudi intelligence, Prince Turki bin Faysal, revealed that a Saudi Shi'i, Ahmad Mughassil, was the mastermind behind the bombing and that he was believed to be in Iran. Moreover, at the end of March, the Canadian government presented evidence that another Saudi Shi'i, Hani 'Abd al-Rahim al-Sayigh, detained in Ottawa, was also involved in the al-Khobar explosion. In April, U.S. and Saudi intelligence officials further linked Brig. Ahmad Sharifi, a top official of Iran's Islamic Revolutionary Guard Corps, to al-Sayigh and the bomb attack.

After being deported from Canada to the United States, al-Sayigh agreed initially to cooperate with U.S. authorities. When he decided not to talk, however, he was deported to Saudi Arabia, as the Saudis claimed to have hard evidence against him.

Riyadh was reluctant to cooperate with Washington on the investigation, however. The Saudi rapprochement with Iran was most likely dictating Riyadh's policy, as Saudi officials did not want to provide evidence that would lead the United States to retaliate against Iran. Although Prince Nayif said in March 1998 that the investigation was complete and that results would shortly be forthcoming, no announcement has yet been made.

Containing the Opposition: The Al Sa'ud's Struggle with Dissent

Different types of opposition, one mainstream Sunni and the other minority Shi'i, necessitated different Saudi containment policies. The regime moved to shore up religious support where it existed. To assuage the Sunni majority, King Fahd created a Consultative Council in March 1992, and sixty members were appointed in August 1993; the council expanded to ninety in July 1997. To placate the Shi'i minority as well, three additional Shi'is were appointed in 1997 to join the one originally appointed to the 1993 council.

The regime's moves signified the increasing importance Fahd attached to legitimation of the government by the religious establishment in the face of the radical fundamentalists' ongoing threat. The establishment 'ulama found it easiest to condemn the overseas-based CDLR rather than the Awakening Shaykhs at home, while the government-controlled press initiated a smear campaign against the Awakening Shaykhs.

The government relied on General Mufti Bin Baz for his legitimizing views, but the growing assertiveness of the establishment 'ulama worried the regime. Indeed, the radical and establishment 'ulama increasingly seemed to share similar educational experiences and hold similar views. Disappointed with the Council of Senior 'Ulama, King Fahd announced in October 1994 the creation of a Supreme Council of Islamic Affairs and a Council for Islamic Mission and Guidance, both of which were designed to marginalize the establishment 'ulama.

In the 1990s, the Saudi government also realized that accommodating the Shi'i opposition could easily temper a serious conflict. Both the government and the Shi'i opposition seemed to have greatly desired an arrangement, which was agreed to by Tawfiq al-Shaykh, a leader of the Saudi Shi'i opposition in exile, and King Fahd in 1993. As a result of the agreement, many exiled Saudi Shi'is returned to the Eastern Province, but both sides kept the news of the agreement fairly quiet for fear that too much publicity would draw fire from the Sunni radical fundamentalists.

Conclusion: Saudi Arabia, the Opposition, and Crown Prince 'Abdallah

The growth of the post–1991 Gulf War radical fundamentalist movement represented both continuity and a departure for Saudi Arabia. Centrifugal forces have plagued the Al Sa'ud since the state's formation, but the new opposition went so far as to question the regime's Islamic legitimacy. Centralizing Islamic institutions was part of the Saudi process of state building, but under King Fahd the radical Sunni fundamentalists perceived a manifest contradiction between the Islamic image the government sought to project and the reality they saw. It was more they could stomach.

Since November 1995, however, Crown Prince 'Abdallah has been king of Saudi Arabia in all but name, and opposition activity has generally subsided. Projecting an image of a simple and pious man, 'Abdallah appears to be more acceptable to Saudi Arabia's Islamic opposition than is King Fahd. 'Abdallah has been particularly active in working to change economic conditions, and under his leadership, Saudi Arabia has made some adjustments to address the economic realities of unstable petroleum revenues.

Many in Saudi Arabia have high hopes that 'Abdallah can realign Saudi foreign policy and balance between the modern and the religious. He may well be able to restore the balance of "Faysal's order." He has introduced the Internet to Saudi Arabia and has sparked debates on such controversial topics as incoming tourism and increasing rights for women. As for tradition, as the country celebrated its centenary in January 1999, Crown Prince 'Abdallah let the religious establishment flex its muscles and publicly oppose some aspects of the celebrations. He recognizes that Islamic legitimacy is central to the rule of the Al Sa'ud, but he has also tried to accommodate the opposition and has freed several jailed 'ulama.

Yet, social discontent continues, and whereas it does not always breed radical Islamic fundamentalism, it can certainly be a contributing factor. The modern Saudi state, since its founding by Ibn Sa'ud in 1902, has always been able to handle domestic political challenges. But even times of calm are not entirely without opposition activity.

The key lesson for foreigners concerned with the future of the kingdom is that closer attention must be paid to religious trends within and outside the religious establishment. A hidden struggle continues regarding who will determine the Wahhabi da'wa. One must read for oneself what dissidents write and listen to their taped talks. Although the subject matter is sometimes difficult for foreigners, the Saudi royal family and westernized liberal Saudis are not always the best interpreters of this material. Saudi countermeasures are also worthy of attention. The Al Sa'ud is not quick to acknowledge dissent, but the increase of discord in Islamic institutions, particularly those concerning da'wa, is a signal that the leadership is worried.

Chapter 1
The Nature of Radical Islamic Fundamentalism in Saudi Arabia

Saudi Arabia has long projected a public image as the one Islamic country that has perfected a unique and successful combination of tradition and modernity. Since the Persian Gulf War, however, social and economic problems have plagued the country and have led to the rise of a radical Islamic fundamentalist movement that has challenged this public Saudi persona. The movement is an agglomeration of groups and trends with no acknowledged leader, although several of the groups profess appreciation for two *ulama* (religious leaders), known as the "Awakening Shaykhs," who were released in late June 1999 after nearly five years in a Saudi jail.

Unlike the formation of other tribal states in the Arabian peninsula, the formation of Saudi Arabia after World War I involved the unique harnessing of the Wahhabi *da'wa* (creed[1])—the radical reformist philosophy of the followers of Muhammad bin 'Abd al-Wahhab and the founders of the first Saudi state in the eighteenth century—in the service of the political aims of the Al Sa'ud, the Saudi family. Like any other elite involved in state formation, the Al Sa'ud was forced to deal with the cardinal issues of relations between the state and society, and between the state and other states. But the kingdom's unique founding circumstances—in which one ruling family formed an alliance with the leader of a reforming Islamic creed—dictated that politics in Saudi Arabia would be conducted in the shadow of Wahhabism, and that the Wahhabi 'ulama would have an important role in the determination of Saudi policies.

1

Saudi Arabia is popularly perceived as the most religious of all the Arab countries, but the nature of Islam in Saudi Arabia—or rather the question of who determines the dominant Islamic discourse—has been the subject of controversy since the founding of the state. Although not always in the foreground, the controversy has appeared often during crises over foreign policy, education, modernization, and the country's Shi'i population. Over the years, economic and political grievances have often been added to the agenda of those posing a challenge to Islam, Saudi-style.

The Ideological Dimension

The ideologies of modern Islamic movements have been the subject of several attempts to generate an agreed-upon nomenclature. The various terms each emphasize a different dimension. "Islamism," for instance, suggests an all-encompassing ideology, whereas the term "political Islam" suggests a movement to bring Islam to the center of politics.[2] R. Hrair Dekmejian states that "the most appropriate term" for the "revivalist phenomenon" is one of the terms used by the adherents themselves, *al-usuliyya al-Islamiyya* (Islamic fundamentalism), "since it connotes a search for the fundamentals of the faith, the foundations of the Islamic community and polity (*umma*), and the bases of legitimate authority (*shar'iyyat al-hukm*)."[3]

In the Saudi case, it is official Islam that is fundamentalist, in that the country claims to be governed by the fundamentals of Islamic law—the Qur'an and the *sunna* (deeds and sayings) of the Prophet—without *bid'a* (accrued "non-Islamic" practices or innovations). The official 'ulama affirm this in their pronouncements, as well as by the very fact that they—the inheritors of the fundamentalist Wahhabi da'wa—serve in the government and defend the regime.

The subject of this study, the antiestablishment Islamic movement in Saudi Arabia, is best described as a radical fundamentalist movement. It is led by 'ulama raised and educated within the state fundamentalist system, but it is radical in that it attacks the Saudi royal family and the official 'ulama for not being fundamentalist *enough*, and for having abandoned the true fundamentalist path. Interestingly, as its followers are supremely confident in their level of Islamic learning, they do not feel a need to call upon the name of Muhammad bin 'Abd al-Wahhab for legitimation; this may also be because the establishment 'ulama and the Saudi state have so coopted and perhaps even tainted his persona that the name of Bin 'Abd al-Wahhab no longer performs for the radicals the task of a legitimizing touchstone.[4]

It should be emphasized that, unlike most Sunni radical fundamentalist leaders (such as Abu A'la Mawdudi, Hasan al-Banna, Sayyid Qutb, and Hasan al-Turabi), the leaders of Saudi Arabia's radical Sunni fundamentalist movement are not laymen but rather 'ulama, rebelling against the very fundamentalist system that created them. Although the movement's roots are in the establishment 'ulama, its leadership does not come from the establishment's higher ranks. Ironically, this makes the radical Sunni opposition more like its antithesis, the Shi'i Islamic movement, whose leadership is also composed of 'ulama. As for the rank-and-file of the movement, it is composed mostly of educated members of the middle class.

The radical Sunni opposition in Saudi Arabia shares some features with other radical Islamists, particularly an alienation from and a skepticism of the official 'ulama. Emmanuel Sivan, in his seminal work *Radical Islam*, stresses that radicals in Egypt and Syria take the establishment to task for giving approval to government initiatives deemed contrary to the *shari'a* (Islamic law). "What is lacking," wrote one Islamist quoted by Sivan, "are ulama free of chains of office, function, and dependence, ulama who cannot be hired and fired at will, and [who] are economically independent, hence impervious to pressures."[5] Furthermore, as noted by Sa'id Hawwa, the ideologue of the Syrian Muslim Brotherhood, "many an ignoramus sheikh considers opposition to any political regime a sin smacking of Kharijite heresy. One realizes how boorish are such ulama when one considers that[,] if they are right, then Abraham and Moses have sinned in resisting Nimrod and Pharaoh. . . ."[6]

According to the Saudi radical fundamentalists, the arrival in the kingdom of Muslim Brotherhood activists fleeing the regime of Egyptian president Gamal Abdel Nasser in the 1950s and 1960s gave impetus to those dissatisfied with the religious status quo in Saudi Arabia. They presented a tradition of Islamic activism that combined with the revivalist ideas of Bin 'Abd al-Wahhab to produce "a unique model of mature Islamic activism which found political expression during and after the Gulf crisis."[7]

A change of generations has also apparently been a factor in the growth of radical fundamentalism. Younger scholars, influenced by the ideas of Islamic activism and impatient with the elder 'ulama, created Islamic study circles that developed in the 1980s. Of particular note among these scholars were 'A'id Al-Qarni, 'Awad Al-Qarni, Nasir Al-'Umar (the latter was released from jail in June 1999), and the two stars of post–Gulf War radical fundamentalism, Salman bin Fahd al-'Awda and Safar bin 'Abd al-Rahman al-Hawali (the Awakening Shaykhs). What made these men unique was their ability to combine Islamic learning with an appreciation of current affairs and implications for Muslims worldwide. Moreover, they enjoyed good relations with mainstream official scholars, despite differences of opinion. It was this relationship, combined with the fact that they did not present an overt political agenda, that initially sheltered the young scholars from persecution by the state.[8]

Sources of Discontent: The Social and Economic Roots of Postwar Radical Sunni Fundamentalism

The rise of Islamic movements in the Middle East has been widely studied.[9] In general, the movements are a response to modernization not in its technological sense, but as a reaction to the lack of economic and social progress it promised. As scholar Nazih Ayubi wrote in *Political Islam*, "The Islamists are not angry because the airplane has replaced the camel; they are angry because they cannot get on the airplane."[10] Despite providing burgeoning educational programs, many regimes have failed to provide sufficient opportunities for employment or social advancement. Islamic movements thus provide a mechanism to defend values against the perceived threat of modernity. As an all-encompassing ideology, Islamic fundamentalism promises a solution to all of society's ills. It also has the advantage of presenting itself as an authentic ideology, one ostensibly not imported from and contaminated by the West.[11]

The social and economic conditions that gave rise to Islamic fundamentalism elsewhere in the Middle East also exist in Saudi Arabia, where "frustrated expectations" may be greater because of the promise of oil wealth. Yet, Saudis are economically more prosperous than many other groups in the Arab world. It is important to note, therefore, an important difference: Saudi Muslims perceive themselves as living in the cradle of Islam. They bask in the glow of the Holy Ka'ba and are able to pray daily at the prophet's mosque in Medina. More than any other regime, the Saudi government asserts its right to rule in the name of Islam. To emphasize this point, in 1986 King Fahd took the title *Khadim al-Haramayn al-Sharifayn* (servant of the Two Holy Shrines, in Mecca and Medina), a title previously reserved for the caliph. When Saudi Muslims perceive that their government is no longer ruling according to Islam as they define it, the cognitive dissonance is magnified, and the situation is ripe for radical fundamentalism.

Economic Woes and the Demographic Bind

Saudi Arabia is what is known as a "rentier state." Its income comes not from taxes, but rather from the income (rents) on a commodity—in this case, petroleum products. The government distributes much of its oil income to its citizens rather than collecting a portion of the citizens' income. Saudi Arabia has an informal "social contract" with its subjects: the government provides a cradle-to-grave welfare system and employment in the public sector, and, in exchange, the people forgo their right to representation in the government.

In the boom years of high oil prices, this arrangement operated relatively smoothly. But with the slide in oil prices

in the mid- and late 1980s, Saudi Arabia, like other Gulf countries, began to experience difficult economic periods. Income
from oil revenues dropped from nearly $118 billion in 1981
to only $18 billion in 1986, but it rose on the eve of the Gulf
War in 1990 to $40 billion.[12] Similarly, Saudi gross domestic
product (GDP) dropped from $155.1 billion in 1981 to $73.2
billion in 1986, but it rose again to $104.7 billion in 1990.[13]

This situation might have been considered manageable
had Saudi Arabia's population not risen so dramatically. With
a population of about 9.8 million in 1981, it had a per capita
GDP of $15,810. But its sizable population-growth rate pro-
duced a population of 13.4 million in 1986, lowering its per
capita GDP to only $5,479. In 1990, with a population of 14.9
million, the per capita GDP rose slightly to $7,039. By com-
parison, in the United States the GDP per capita was $13,551
in 1981, $18,374 in 1986, and $22,983 in 1990.[14]

Additionally, Saudi Arabia's high rate of population
growth led to an age distribution pyramid severely weighted
toward the young. For example, in 1990 on the eve of the
Gulf War, 49 percent of Saudis were under the age of 20,
whereas in France the percentage was only 28, and in the
United States it was only 29.[15] Although the Saudi government does not provide unemployment statistics, Western
sources usually place the figure around 25 percent.[16]

Near the beginning of the Gulf War, the Saudi government was finding it increasingly difficult to provide the services
the population had come to expect, and, as in other Islamic
countries, the Islamists were filling the void. For instance, the
Charitable Fund for Assisting Youths' Marriages was active in
helping many Saudis who could no longer afford a marriage
dowry, the wedding party, and the furniture needed to start a
new home. Saudi women needed wedding dresses, and the
charity provided for these needs as well. The organization
was run by "bearded men in short robes and untied head
scarves"—the garb of Saudi founder Ibn Sa'ud's militant
Ikhwan (radical tribal followers of the Wahhabi da'wa) and of
many modern radical fundamentalists in Saudi Arabia.[17]

The Higher Education Trap

As part of the bargain that involved the political marginalization of the 'ulama (discussed below), the regime gave the clerics a major voice in education, including higher education. This agreement resulted in a strong fundamentalist influence in Saudi education, even at those universities not specifically designated as "Islamic," because the teachers of Islamic subjects were often Islamists from Egypt and other countries. The arrangement also created a powerful mix of a generally literate elite and a secularly educated 'ulama with a fundamentalist message. Post–Gulf War radical Sunni fundamentalism was largely the work of people at universities, where networks developed that crossed tribal and regional lines.[18]

The growth in educational institutions at home led to a reluctance to send Saudis abroad, particularly to the United States, to study. The number of Saudis studying abroad reached a peak of more than 12,500 in the mid-1980s but then dropped to 3,554 in 1990 and was only slightly more than 3,400 in 1996.[19] In general, the Saudi government does not now fund education abroad for disciplines or programs taught at home. Although studying in the West does not guarantee the inculcation of secular or liberal values, it does seem that the increasing number of students who remained at home, studying in the insular Saudi system, provided a fertile ground for the development of radical Sunni fundamentalism.

Higher education is free in Saudi Arabia. A university diploma is prestigious, and therefore the authorities are reluctant to disadvantage candidates by turning them away. Yet, performance standards have been lowered to allow anyone to graduate from the system. Prior to the economic slowdown of the mid-1980s, a diploma guaranteed government employment; at the beginning of the twenty-first century, however, it is becoming more difficult to find work for all. Many Saudi students choose as their major course of study the arts and humanities—a sure ticket to unemployment. The opening of new technical and vocational schools has failed to attract large numbers of students, as technical work is considered menial and does not pay as well as the anticipated white-collar job.[20]

Tribal Frustration

Much of the leadership and the rank-and-file membership of the radical Sunni fundamentalist movement continues to identify itself or be identified tribally. One commentator noted that "recently urbanized bedouin" have become converts to the Islamic cause, catalyzed by a feeling of relative deprivation.[21] The literature of the opposition demonstrates a keen awareness of tribal sensitivities and of the tribal component in the identity of many of its supporters. Although it is doubtful that the tribal resentment of the Saudi government as portrayed by some in the opposition—notably the Committee for the Defense of Legitimate Rights (CDLR)—is invented, it is difficult to assess the extent and effect of this resentment, or whether the CDLR has exaggerated it for its own purposes.

CDLR literature describes many examples of tribal frustration. For example, when it reported the arrest of Dr. Husayn Mashhur al-Hazimi, professor of physics at King Saud University, the CDLR noted that al-Hazimi was a member of the famous Hawazim tribe and that his father, Shaykh Muhammad, was a chief of the tribe and an important figure in Jizan province. The CDLR protested the arrests of several tribal members, including one from the very prominent Shammar tribe. Protests by tribal leaders, the CDLR noted, were "indicative of the increasing anger of the tribes." The organization was so intent on showing tribal discontent in Saudi Arabia that it emphasized its announcement that Kassab al-Rashid, "from the tribe of 'Utayba," had joined the CDLR office in London.[22]

The CDLR has emphasized the humiliation of the tribes by labeling the Al Sa'ud as an uneducated, unqualified band of upstarts who trampled the honor of more qualified people and of the ordinary citizen.[23] It has also reported countless incidents involving individuals bearing tribal eponyms, such as Ghamidi, 'Utaybi, and Shammari. For example, the organization reported a "campaign of terror" against "the people of the north"—all of the Shammar tribe. In another example, the government reportedly dismissed from their posts the 'ulama of the Qahtan, Ghamid, and Bani Shihr tribes. Another CDLR report noted that "approximately 10,000" bedouins of the Harb tribe were forbidden to enter an area of Qasim because it had been declared a private hunting ground of the defense minster, Prince Sultan bin 'Abd al-'Aziz.[24] The CDLR further reported that the Saudi ambassador to the United States, Prince Bandar bin Sultan, "spoke in an ugly manner about the 'Utayba tribe" because one of its members, Shaykh Kassab Al-'Utaybi, had fled the country.[25]

In further CDLR claims, the organization maintained that three Mutayri members of that bastion of Wahhabi conservatism, the *hay'at al-amr bil-ma'ruf wal-nahy 'an al-munkar* (the Committee for the Enjoining of Good and the Prevention of Evil)—known abroad as the religious police—had been arrested for uncovering the corruption of an officer related to a high-ranking Interior Ministry official; that the al-Muqbil family of Burayda reportedly wrote to the CDLR to clarify that a judge who had been condemned by the committee was not their relative or from their tribe, the Subay'; and that the Mutayr tribe of Hafr al-Batin was reportedly outraged after one of their sons, an officer in the special security forces, had been forced into retirement just days before he was eligible for a promotion.[26] In addition, said the CDLR, the Qahtan had protested in the mosque in Khamis Mushayt against confiscation of large tracts of land belonging to the tribe.[27] M.S. Zayn Al-'Abdin, seeming to echo opposition sentiments, wrote in a pamphlet that the Al Sa'ud thought the people were their slaves:

> They have displayed that attitude in the identities and passports of citizens of the country: (citizenship: Saudi!). I do not know how the citizenship of a person from the tribe of Qahtan, Mutair, Ajman, Utaiba, Ghamid, Zahran, Sbei', Shummar, or Bani Khaled or others of the famous Arab tribes, yes, I do not know how can their citizenship be Saudi while they themselves claim purer nobility and ancestry than the family of Saud.[28]

Marginalizing the 'Ulama: The Religious Establishment and the State in Saudi Arabia

It has become axiomatic to describe Saudi history as the successful alliance of *din* (religion) and *dawla* (state), of *'ulama* (clerics) and *umara* (princes). The Saudi family provided the religious establishment with positions and funding and allowed the conservative religious and social values of central Arabian society, represented by the 'ulama, to dominate the entire Saudi state. In return, the 'ulama provided the Al Sa'ud with the religious legitimacy needed to rule.

The relationship between the two was actually much more complex than that simple formula. As Saudi society became more modernized and exposed to the West, and as the Al Sa'ud sought a more centralized Saudi state, conflicts arose. The 'ulama represented the conservative elements in society that opposed modernization and wished to continue the kind of decentralized, tribally organized, and consensus-building rule that had existed prior to the establishment of the modern Saudi state. In this struggle, the Al Sa'ud always prevailed, but the family often had to mold its policies to address the concerns of the 'ulama.

At various times in Saudi history, groups of 'ulama—usually from the outer circles of the establishment—have challenged the Al Sa'ud. Beginning in 1902, 'Abd al-'Aziz bin 'Abd al-Rahman Al Sa'ud (Ibn Sa'ud), the founder of the modern Saudi state, harnessed the Wahhabi 'ulama and the tribes they influenced to expand his nascent tribal authority. The vanguard of these forces were the Ikhwan, fanatical tribal followers of the Wahhabi da'wa, whom many of the leading 'ulama supported. They viewed the state as a traditional Arabian chieftaincy, a decentralized amalgam of tribes under one or more leaders. They believed the role of the government was to implement the shari'a, as determined by the 'ulama, and to expand the borders in the name of Wahhabi Islam. The Ikhwan viewed matters of religion as the purview of an independent, decentralized, and nonhierarchical 'ulama; the duty of the ruler was to follow the 'ulama's decisions in all spheres.

Yet for Ibn Saʿud, raised in cosmopolitan Kuwait, the exigencies of *realpolitik* began to impinge on this traditional form of government. The annexation of the equally cosmopolitan area of the Hijaz in 1926 and the British-led state-formation efforts in Transjordan and Iraq beginning in the 1920s forced upon him the need to form a more centralized, modern state. He could no longer countenance Ikhwan fanaticism, which had led to attacks on pilgrims and raids deep into British-held Iraq and Transjordan. His *raison d'état* began to diverge from that of his Wahhabi vanguard. The more conservative ʿulama supported some of the demands of the Ikhwan, but others opposed them. The Ikhwan rebelled, and in the end Ibn Saʿud was forced to confront the Ikhwan on the battlefield, from which he emerged victorious.[29]

With end of the Ikhwan rebellion in 1930, Ibn Saʿud coopted the leading ʿulama into the nascent, modern state system, part of a policy that one scholar has termed "encapsulation." The new state structure engulfed the ʿulama in an amoeba-like embrace and controlled them, yet the ʿulama provided no rubber stamp for Saudi policies. Ibn Saʿud made the senior ʿulama the arbiters of the Wahhabi daʿwa and established Wahhabi Islam as the state religion. The religious opinions of the senior ʿulama would be the only ones to carry weight, but the interests of the state, as defined by the king, would take precedence. "Wahhabi Islam thus [became] a moral code, a unifying factor and ideological motivator of society, but only in accordance with state interests and by legitimizing royal Saudi rule."[30] Only the most senior ʿulama, however, were coopted. An antiestablishment, centrifugal group of ʿulama remained whose ideological descendants would appear repeatedly in Saudi history.

As the Saudi state became more bureaucratized, incorporation of the ʿulama into the state administration diminished their role. They became instead a simple pressure group, never acting as an autonomous center of power. The effect was the normalization "of the use of religion and the religious establishment as a source of legitimacy."[31] In exchange for their role in legitimizing Al Saʿud rule, however, the ʿulama

were given extensive responsibilities in areas important to
them, including the judiciary; religious education; guidance
and the spread of Islam overseas; the *hay'at al-amr bil-ma'ruf
wal-nahy 'an al-munkar* (Committee for the Enjoining of Good
and the Prevention of Evil); and the *da'irat al-buhuth
al-Islamiyya, al-ifta, al-da'wa wal-irshad* (Directorate for Religious Research, Rulings, Mission, and Guidance). Although
the 'ulama were allowed a considerable degree of autonomy
in managing these institutions, the king retained final authority,[32] further "encapsulating" the 'ulama into roles clearly
defined by the state. By the 1950s, the 'ulama were firmly in
their place as paid civil servants, hired and fired by the king.
The king was the *imam*, the leader of the Wahhabi faithful;
the elite 'ulama would have large sway over purely religious
matters but would be kept out of politics. This led to the replacement of the umara–'ulama alliance with one between
the umara and the *khubara*, or technocrats.[33]

For the radical Sunni fundamentalists who would protest
these events, this last development was the cardinal sin, rep-
resenting the imposition by the royal family of "un-Islamic
concepts" on the thinking of the official 'ulama. The most
important and "un-Islamic" of these concepts, as the opposition put it, was that "those in charge know best as to the
interests of the nation." Nevertheless, this arrangement became an accepted norm and social convention.[34]

Notes

1. The word *da'wa* can mean creed or call and is most often translated
   as proselytizing or missionizing; but to engage in *da'wa* more properly conveys the act of preaching, summoning the people to lead a
   proper Islamic way of life, and pointing out the means to achieve
   true Islamic society and government.

2. William Shepard, "Islam and Ideology: Towards a Typology," *International Journal of Middle Eastern Studies* [*IJMES*] 19 (1987), pp. 307–338.
   Shepard, who has dealt with the issue of classifying movements of
   political Islam, is correct in pointing out the dangers of labeling, cau-
   tioning that one should think of these labels as "Weberian 'ideal types,'
   that is[,] analytical constructs which may or may not correspond in
   detail to actual cases but which help us analyze and compare a large
   number of cases." (p. 307.)

3. R. Hrair Dekmejian, "Islamic Revival: Catalysts, Categories, and Consequences," in Shireen Hunter, ed., *The Politics of Islamic Revival* (Bloomington: Indiana University Press, 1988), pp. 3–19.

4. For more on the fact that the radicals do not call on Bin 'Abd al-Wahhab for legitimation, see Madawi Al-Rasheed, "La couronne et le turban: l'état saoudien à recherche d'une nouvelle légitimité" [The Crown and the Turban: The Saudi State in Search of a New Legitimacy], in Bassma Kodmani-Darwish and May Chartouni-Dubarry, eds., *Les états Arabes face à la contestation Islamique* [The Arab States Face an Islamic Challenge] (Paris: Armand Colin, 1997), pp. 71–97, particularly p. 74.

5. Emmanuel Sivan, *Radical Islam: Medieval Theology and Modern Politics* (New Haven, Conn.: Yale University Press, 1985), p. 14.

6. Ibid., p. 105. The Kharijites (in Arabic, *Khawarij*) were one of Islam's earliest sects who violently attacked all those who disagreed with them, branding them infidels. The name means "those who went out," and is an epithet accusing them of having abandoned the community of believers. Its use today mean that a person or group has made irresponsible accusations against the ruling authority and has therefore left the community of the faithful.

7. See Movement for Islamic Reform in Arabia (MIRA), *History of Dissent: The Story of Islamic Dissent in Arabia*, chapter 2, "Social Transformation and Political Explosion," online at http://www.miraserve.com/chap2.html.

8. Ibid.

9. Among the best studies of the Islamic revival are Nazih Ayubi, *Political Islam: Religion and Politics in the Arab World* (London: Routledge, 1991) and Sivan, *Radical Islam.*

10. Ayubi, *Political Islam*, pp. 176–177.

11. See the editor's introduction in Meir Litvak, ed., *Islam and Democracy in the Arab World* (Tel Aviv: Dayan Center, ha-Kibbutz ha-Meuhad, 1997), pp. 9–23.

12. All dollar values are in current dollars. *Organization of Petroleum Exporting Countries (OPEC) Annual Bulletin* (Vienna: OPEC, 1996)

13. International Monetary Fund [IMF], *International Financial Statistics Yearbook, 1998* (Washington: IMF, 1998, hereafter cited as *Statistics Yearbook*); IMF, "International Financial Statistics, November 1998" (Washington: IMF, 1998, hereafter cited as "Statistics, November 1998").

14. *Statistics Yearbook, 1998*; "Statistics, November 1998." Saudi Arabia has one of the highest rates of population increase in the world: 3.4 percent in 1990, compared with 0.42 percent for France and 0.8 percent for the United States. U.S. Bureau of the Census, *International Data Base*, online at http://www.census.gov/ipc/www/idbnew.html (hereafter cited as Census IDB).

15. Census IDB.

16. Results of a recent study by King 'Abd Al-'Aziz University put the figure at 27 percent in 1999. "Saudi Unemployment More than Doubles in Six Years," Agence France-Presse, April 10, 1999.

17. *Wall Street Journal*, January 15, 1992; *Wall Street Journal*, January 16, 1992.

18. F. Gregory Gause III, *Oil Monarchies: Domestic and Security Challenges in the Arab Gulf States* (New York: Council on Foreign Relations, 1994), p. 85; Joseph Kostiner, "State, Islam, and Opposition in Saudi Arabia: The Post-Gulf War Phase," *MERIA Journal* (July 1997), online at http://www.biu.ac.il/SOC/besa/meria/journal/1997/issue2/jvln2a8.html. In 1998, 30 percent of Saudi students were studying Islamic studies; religion constituted one-third of the coursework of the other 70 percent; see Patrick Clawson, "Cheap Sheik," *New Republic*, October 26, 1998.

19. *Statistical Yearbooks of Saudi Arabia* for 1979–1994; Saudi Arabia Ministry of Higher Education, online at http://www.mohe.gov.sa.

20. Delwin Roy, "Saudi Arabian Education: Development Policy," *Middle Eastern Studies* 28 (July 1992), pp. 477–508.

21. R. Hrair Dekmejian, "The Rise of Political Islam in Saudi Arabia," *Middle East Journal* 48 (autumn 1994), pp. 627–643.

22. Committee for the Defense of Legitimate Rights (CDLR), *CDLR Communiqué*, no. 8, May 8, 1994; *CDLR Communiqué*, no. 14, August 21, 1994; CDLR, press release, October 2, 1994. CDLR documents are available from the CDLR London office via email request at cdlr@cdlr.net.

23. Publishing tribal grievances may have also been an attempt by the CDLR to garner support from that sector, rather than a reflection of existing support and humiliation by the Al Sa'ud.

24. *CDLR Monitor*, no. 30, January 13, 1995; *CDLR Monitor*, no. 34, February 10, 1995; *CDLR Monitor*, no. 42, April 7, 1995.

25. *CDLR Monitor*, March 29, 1995; *CDLR Monitor*, no. 41, March 31, 1995.

26. *Al-Huquq* 54, June 28, 1995; *CDLR Monitor,* no. 54, June 30, 1995.

27. *Al-Huquq* 59, August 2, 1995; *CDLR Monitor,* no. 59, August 4, 1995.

28. M.S. Zein Al-Abdin, "The Saudi Terror" (Birmingham, England: Center of Islamic Studies, February 1995), pamphlet.

29. Joseph Kostiner, *The Making of Saudi Arabia, 1916–1936: From Chieftaincy to Monarchical State* (New York: Oxford University Press, 1993), pp. 116–140.

30. Kostiner, "State, Islam, and Opposition in Saudi Arabia."

31. Ayman Al-Yassini, *Religion and State in the Kingdom of Saudi Arabia* (Boulder, Colo.: Westview, 1985), pp. 67-68.

32. Yassini, pp. 59–79.

33. Al-Rasheed, "La couronne et le turban," pp. 71–97, particularly p. 74. James Piscatori described the process in which administrative decrees, usually termed *nizam*—as opposed to *qanun*, which has a secular connotation—have been used to supplement or circumvent the *shari'a.* Thus the Western-influence Ottoman commercial code was introduced in 1931 and revised in 1954. James Piscatori, "Ideological Politics in Saudi Arabia," in James Piscatori, ed., *Islam in the Political Process* (Cambridge, Mass.: Cambridge University Press, 1983), pp. 62–63.

34. See MIRA, *History of Dissent,* chapter 2.

Faysal's Order

I t was Saudi Arabia's third king, Faysal bin 'Abd al-'Aziz, who developed the current modus operandi between the *'ulama* (religious leaders) and the state, part of a multifaceted system governing state–society relations termed "Faysal's order."[1] Faysal, who ruled as king from 1964 to 1975 but had been prime minister before that, sought to establish the kingdom as a modern yet conservative society. He sought to harness new oil-based wealth to expand the military and establish the Al Sa'ud as military defender, provider of social welfare, and main economic force in the country. These intentions were accompanied by massive technological innovation, investment in infrastructure, and an intensive bureaucratization.[2]

Importantly, oil wealth enabled Faysal to establish a new "social contract" with the Saudi people. He could raise the standard of living and provide free education and a cradle-to-grave welfare system to benefit all, compensating those conservatives offended by modernization. In return, it was expected that those who benefited would not demand political participation.

The Development of the Religious Establishment

Faysal met the standards expected of Saudi kings. He was an imam, personally pious, and he defended the kingdom. He gave the 'ulama their say but safely encapsulated them in the new Ministry of Justice. His goal was a modern society that was socioculturally traditional and religiously conservative.[3] In pursuit of this purpose, he had the support of the establishment 'ulama. By channeling the 'ulama away from politics and into civil service, Faysal effectively limited their independence. When General Mufti Shaykh Muhammad bin Ibrahim bin 'Abd al-Latif Al al-Shaykh died in 1969, Faysal did not replace him. The position remained vacant until the 1990s. The Ministry of Justice was established in 1970, and in 1974 and 1975, the *shar'i* (Islamic law–based) judicial system was reorganized along Western lines, with summary courts, general courts, and courts of causation. The judges in these courts are officially independent and, according to the law, cannot be discharged from their posts.

During Faysal's reign and afterward, several quasi-judicial bodies were established ostensibly to supplement the *shari'a* (Islamic law), but they actually restricted it. These committees and boards handle a range of issues, particularly commercial and labor disputes, and can render decisions following Islamic, Western, or international law. Professionally trained lawyers staff these bodies. Administrative regulations and royal decrees frequently do not follow the shari'a, leading to many deviations from Islamic practice. For instance, the Social Insurance Law introduced in 1970 does not adhere to the Islamic laws of inheritance following the death of an insured worker.[4]

Another important governmental body is the *diwan al-mazalim* (Board of Grievances). Directly answerable to the king, this organization is an extrapolation of the tribal institution known as the *majlis* (council), through which people would bring their complaints to the ruler. The board existed informally in Saudi Arabia until 1954, when it was made a department in the Saudi Cabinet. In 1955, it was made an independent body under the direct control of the king.[5]

The true power of the 'ulama rests with two bodies. Faysal established the *majlis hay'at kibar al-'ulama* (the Council of Senior 'Ulama) in 1971 with the country's top *'alim* (Islamic scholar), 'Abd al-'Aziz Bin Baz, as its leader.[6] The council issues *fatwas* (religious edicts) mostly on matters submitted by the government. Membership is prestigious and determined by appointment of the king.[7] In addition to the Council of Senior 'Ulama, there is the Standing Committee on Religious Pronouncement (*ifta*), consisting of four members of the council selected by the king. Administratively, this committee is part of *al-ri'asa al-'amma lil-idarat al-buhuth al-'ilmiyya wal-ifta' wal-da'wa wal-irshad* (the General Presidency for Religious Research, Religious Pronouncement, Preaching, and Guidance). Bin Baz was the head of the General Presidency, the Council of Senior 'Ulama, and the Standing Committee.[8] Faysal's creation of these bodies completed the centralizing process, making religion dependent on the central authority of the state, but centrifugal forces remained, and not all were happy with the new state of affairs.

The Islamic Challenge to Faysal's Order

Indeed, Faysal's orders did not go entirely unchallenged. Conservative forces opposed his decision to introduce television to the kingdom in 1963 when he was crown prince, and some 'ulama took to the streets in protest. In September 1965, demonstrators tried to storm the TV station in Riyadh and were shot by the police. One of those killed in what some Arab newspapers described as an "abortive Islamic coup d'état" was Khalid bin Musa'id bin 'Abd al-'Aziz, Faysal's nephew. Despite the clash, the royal family instituted regular TV broadcasts in 1967.[9]

The Attack on the Meccan Grand Mosque

On November 20, 1979, which corresponded to 1 Muharram 1400, the first day of the new Islamic century, Juhayman bin Muhammad al-'Utaybi and Muhammad bin 'Abdallah al-Qahtani led several hundred men in taking control of the Meccan Haram during the *hajj*, an event one commentator called "The Return of the Ikhwan."[10] The men had tribal roots, and Juhayman's grandfather, a member of the *Ikhwan* (radical tribal followers of the Wahhabi creed), had been killed by Ibn Sa'ud's forces at the battle of Sibila in March 1929. Al-'Utaybi had served for eighteen years in the tribally based *al-Haras al-Watani* (the Saudi Arabian National Guard, or SANG), commanded by 'Abdallah, the current crown prince. Although not 'ulama, the two leaders of the attack had studied under the establishment 'ulama at the Islamic University in Medina. Al-Qahtani was to be proclaimed the Muslim *mahdi* (awaited one) by the Muslim world during the takeover. Al-'Utaybi and al-Qahtani's followers were a rag-tag bunch of Saudis, Egyptian, Kuwaitis, Pakistanis, and Yemenis, and most Saudis did not take their views very seriously. Looking back at their demands from the perspective of post–Gulf War Saudi Arabia, however, their goals seem oddly familiar.

In his writings published before the attack, al-'Utaybi manifested an extreme reaction to Faysal's order. He challenged the Saudis regarding their alliance with "Christians" and demanded the expulsion of all foreign military and civilian experts from the country, as well as the end of diplomatic relations with the corrupt West. He opposed the use of photography and television and upbraided the establishment 'ulama for supporting a degenerate regime. He also specifically attacked leading establishment cleric, Bin Baz: "[He] may know his *sunna* [a fundamental basis of Islamic law] well enough, but he uses it to bolster corrupt rulers." Al-'Utaybi further wrote that Bin Baz was in league with the corrupt Al Sa'ud, and added, "We owe obedience only to those who lead by God's book. Those who lead the Muslims with differing laws and systems and who only take from religion what suits them have no claim on our obedience and their mandate to rule is nil."[11] Importantly, when al-'Utaybi and his followers were detained for questioning in the summer of 1978, Bin Baz refused to label their acts treasonous. Another prominent establishment 'alim, Salih bin Luhaydan, reportedly encouraged the group, whose members were released when they promised to end their activities. The behavior of the establishment 'ulama suggested, it seems, a partial intersecting of views between the radicals and the establishment, and the wish on the part of these 'ulama and the regime to avoid confrontation.

Despite their promise, the rebels attacked the Grand Mosque—the holiest site in Islam—the next year and the Saudi regime turned to the establishment 'ulama to issue a fatwa against al-'Utaybi's group and sanction their removal by force from the Meccan Haram. Although the attack on the mosque occurred on November 20, and the fatwa indicates that the 'ulama received the matter for consideration on the same day, the 'ulama did not issue the fatwa until November 24, just before midnight. This delay has led observers to postulate that the 'ulama were not initially in agreement over what to do and had argued either about the agenda of the group or the propriety of using force in the Haram. Presumably, if the 'ulama, as a body, had shared the same sense of urgency as the royal family, the ruling would have been immediate.

Fatwas traditionally begin with a question that the 'ulama proceed to answer. In this case, "King Khalid asked our opinion of them [al-'Utaybi's group] and what should be done with them." The 'ulama studiously avoided responding to any of the group's accusations about the establishment 'ulama or the regime. They confined their opinion to the acknowledgment that the group had committed a crime by invading the Haram and, by doing so, sought to divide Muslims. As a result, the 'ulama decided that the group's members should be hunted down; if they did not surrender, they were to be killed.[12]

Although the establishment 'ulama were obviously aware of al-'Utaybi's activities prior to the attack, the fatwa was not an outright condemnation. It is reasonable to assume, therefore, that some of the establishment 'ulama—angry about losing their influence in Saudi society—may have sympathized with the group's agenda. Such sentiments, however, were not enough to overcome their loyalty to the Saudi state and to the order established by Faysal. Here, then, was the difference between the radical fundamentalists and the establishment religious forces: They shared concerns, but differed on how the issues should be addressed.

Most Saudis were satisfied with Faysal's order; moreover, al-'Utaybi's group lacked a comprehensive vision. "Their extremism eroded their chances of success and barred them from gaining the sympathy of the general public . . . [T]heir armed intrusion into the Sacred Mosque could never have been condoned by the public[,] irrespective of the motives behind it."[13] The execution of al-'Utaybi, al-Qahtani, and their followers, however, did not end challenges to the Islamic credentials of the regime. The appeal of the radical fundamentalist Saudi 'ulama grew in the 1980s, finding particularly fertile ground among lower-income Sunnis suffering from the economic recession caused by the fall in Saudi oil revenues. Although there were some arrests of Sunni radicals, the 1980s was mostly a time of Shi'i opposition activities inspired by the Islamic Revolution in Iran. In August 1988, the Council of Senior 'Ulama issued a fatwa permitting the execution of four Saudi Shi'is believed to be responsible for the murder of three police officers in the majority Shi'i Eastern Province. In 1989, Saudi Shi'is attacked several Saudi targets, particularly overseas. The regime could easily seek common cause with the radical Sunni fundamentalists when it came to the Shi'is, whom many Sunnis viewed as *mushrikin* (polytheists).[14]

Notes

1. The term "Faysal's Order" was coined by Joseph Kostiner and first appears in Joseph Kostiner and Joshua Teitelbaum, "State Formation and the Saudi Monarchy," in Joseph Kostiner, ed., *Middle Eastern Monarchies: The Challenge of Modernity* (Boulder: Lynne Reiner, 2000), pp. 131–149.

2. Faysal founded twenty government ministries.

3. Kostiner and Teitelbaum, "State Formation and the Saudi Monarchy."

4. Aharon Layish, "'Ulama and Politics in Saudi Arabia," in Metin Heper and Raphael Israeli, eds., *Islam and Politics in the Modern Middle East* (London: Croom Helm, 1984), pp. 29–63. For a recent Saudi view of the kingdom's judiciary, see Ahmed A. Al-Ghadyan, "The Judiciary in Saudi Arabia," *Arab Law Quarterly* 13 (1998), pp. 235–251.

5. Al-Ghadyan, "The Judiciary in Saudi Arabia"; David Long, "The Board of Grievances in Saudi Arabia," *Middle East Journal* 27 (1973), pp. 71–75.

6. Bin Baz died in May 1999 and was replaced by Shaykh 'Abd al-'Aziz bin 'Abdallah Al al-Shaykh.

7. Layish, "'Ulama and Politics in Saudi Arabia,"; Alexander Bligh, "The Saudi Religious Elite (Ulama) as Participant in the Political System of the Kingdom," *International Journal of Middle Eastern Studies* 17 (1985), pp. 37–50.

8. Frank Vogel, "The Complementarity of *Ifta'* and *Qada*': Three Saudi Fatwas on Divorce," in Muhammad Khalil Masud, Brinkley Messnick, and David Powers, eds., *Islamic Legal Interpretation* (Cambridge, Mass.: Harvard University Press, 1996), pp. 262–269. Vogel admits the difficulty in defining *fatwa*-granting institutions, which may arise because of their informal structure and overlapping jurisdictions.

9. Another nephew and full brother of Khalid, Faysal bin Musa'id, described as a religious fanatic avenging his brother's death, assassinated Faysal in 1975. Khalid and Faysal were the children of Ibn Saud's son Musa'id, who had taken Watfa bint Muhammad bin Talal Al Rashid as a wife. Watfa's father was the last ruler of Ha'il, which had been overrun by Ibn Sa'ud in 1921. According to Madawi Al-Rasheed, the author of a study of the Rashidi dynasty, revenge on Faysal was based on lingering Rashidi resentment. Khalid, the Rashidis believed, had not been shot in the demonstration, but assassinated by the Saudi police in his own home. Madawi Al-Rasheed, *Politics in an Arabian Oasis: The Rashidis of Saudi Arabia* (London: I. B. Tauris, 1997), p. 250–252. The mother of Crown Prince 'Abdallah is Fahda, also of the Al Rashid.

10. James Buchan, "The Return of the Ikhwan," in David Holden and Richard Johns, *The House of Saud* (New York: Holt, Rinehart and Winston, 1981), pp. 511–526.

11. Joseph Kechichian, "Islamic Revivalism and Change in Saudi Arabia: Juhayman Al-'Utaybi's 'Letters to the Saudi People,'" *The Muslim World* 80 (1990), pp. 1–16 (containing descriptions, quotes from Juhayman, and analyses of the November 1979 attack on the Meccan Haram).

12. Layish, "'Ulama and Politics in Saudi Arabia"; Mordechai Abir, *Saudi Arabia: Government, Society and the Gulf Crises* (London: Routledge, 1993), pp. 80–82. Joseph Kechichian, "Islamic Revivalism and Change in Saudi Arabia: Juhayman Al-'Utaybi's 'Letters to the Saudi People.'" The fatwa was published in the Foreign Broadcast Information Service Daily Report (FBIS-DR) on November 26, 1979, then by Joseph Kechichian in "The Role of the Ulama in the Politics of an Islamic State: The Case of Saudi Arabia," *International Journal of Middle Eastern Studies* 18 (1986), pp. 53–71; Buchan, "The Return of the Ikhwan," pp. 511–526; Jacob Goldberg, "The Saudi Arabian Kingdom," in Colin Legum et al., eds., *Middle East Contemporary Survey, 1979–1980* (New York: Holmes and Meier, 1981), pp. 681–721; Bligh, "The Saudi Religious Elite." See also *'Ukaz*, November 25–30, 1979.

13. See Movement for Islamic Reform in Arabia (MIRA), *History of Dissent: The Story of Islamic Dissent in Arabia,* chapter 1, "Al Saud, Islam, and the Reform Movement," online at http://www.miraserve.com/chap1.html.

14. Abir, *Saudi Arabia: Government, Society, and the Gulf Crises,* pp. 156–159.

Chapter 3
Loss of Control: Islamic Opposition in the Wake of the Gulf War

The 1991 Persian Gulf War was a vortex in Saudi politics, an event so momentous that it ensnared everything else. Political activists perceived this time to be a fortuitous opportunity to advance their demands. Uncertainty and flux permeated Saudi society during the Gulf crisis:

> Saudi leaders, and society in general, perceived the period of the Gulf crisis as [a] . . . historical crossroad, when the . . . course of development was questioned. This perception resulted from the difficulties of maintaining the old order: there were foreign soldiers on Saudi soil, old concepts of security collapsed, a new strategic alliance with Western states against another Arab state was formed, and the royal family had difficulty ruling the kingdom peacefully. The modernist camp hoped for a change: for more government consideration of Western-style human rights and political representation. On the other hand, the traditionalist–fundamentalists sought to impose a strict Wahhabi value-system on the government and the public.[1]

Saudi 'ulama (religious leaders), both establishment and radical, were shocked to their core by Iraq's invasion of Kuwait and its consequent threat to Saudi Arabia. The role of the Saudi royal family as protector of the kingdom and the holy places would be tested in both groups.

Why did the invasion of Kuwait and the subsequent Gulf War embolden the radical Sunni fundamentalists? In the "social contract" between the royal family and the populace, the rulers were obligated to protect the kingdom. They had previously done so by relying on the "over-the-horizon" U.S. armed forces for protection from aggression. As long as this security guarantee was only implicit and not readily visible, the radical fundamentalists were not motivated to act. But by calling on Christian foreigners to protect them and the holiest places of Islam, the Al Sa'ud had violated their contract. The radical Sunni movement that arose after the invasion played on a sense of humiliation and betrayal apparently felt by many Saudis. It seems that the Gulf War and the angst it brought to many Saudis was another example of what has been termed a "cycle of crisis," a certain urgency, which has been at the root of Islamic resurgences throughout Islamic history, when the *umma* (community of believers) has felt threatened economically, socially, culturally, ideologically, or militarily.[2]

Precursor: The Qarni Incident

In 1989, Prince Khalid Al Faysal, governor of the province of 'Asir, accused 'A'id bin 'Abdallah al-Qarni of sodomy and child molestation. Al-Qarni was a well-known preacher from Abha, in 'Asir, and his publications were distributed by official government agencies.[3] Khalid threw al-Qarni in jail, but a court found him innocent. Thousands traveled to 'Asir in support of the preacher. Once freed, al-Qarni went on a lecture tour of the country, and although such public displays were extremely rare in the kingdom, many Saudis came to see him.[4] The incident highlighted the regime's fear of popular preachers, demonstrating that, in establishment circles, there were individuals like al-Qarni who harbored radical fundamentalist tendencies unpalatable to the government. Al-Qarni's popularity should have also sounded a warning bell for the Al Sa'ud.

Bin Baz's Fatwa on the Acceptance of Non-Muslim Troops

The events surrounding the Council of Senior 'Ulama's issuance of a *fatwa* (religious edict) permitting the arrival of non-Muslim troops in Saudi Arabia during Operations Desert Shield and Desert Storm demonstrated the increased existence of common ground between the establishment 'ulama and the radicals. According to a Saudi student in the United States who interviewed 'ulama and other Saudi officials, the council was reluctant to issue such a fatwa: "It was only after a long discussion with the king and other senior members of the royal family that the most senior Saudi cleric, Shaykh 'Abd al-'Aziz Bin Baz, reluctantly gave his endorsement to the idea on the condition that solid proof be presented as to the threat," said an official of the Royal Court privy to the discussions.[5]

An examination of the fatwa indicates that it was far from explicit and in fact was grudging in tone. It did not mention Americans or Christians, and it stressed only the "need to defend the nation and its constituents by all possible means, and that the duty of those in charge of its affairs is to embark on taking every means that repels that danger . . ." The fatwa continues:

> Therefore, the Council of Senior 'Ulama supports the actions taken by the ruler—may God grant him success—i.e., bringing forces equipped with instruments capable of frightening and terrorizing the one who wants to commit an aggression against this country. This duty is dictated by necessity in the current circumstances and made inevitable by the painful reality. Its legal basis and evidence dictates that the man in charge of the affairs of Muslims should seek the assistance of the one who has the ability to attain the intended.[6]

The Iraqi propaganda machine noticed the half-hearted tone of the fatwa and claimed in radio broadcasts that Bin Baz had been arrested for refusing to approve the decision to bring foreign troops into Saudi Arabia. Within hours of the Iraqi broadcast, Saudi authorities urged Bin Baz to be more explicit in his pronouncement. Saudi radio quoted Bin Baz declaring that "even atheists, Christians, and women deserve appreciation and will be rewarded by God for coming to the defense of the kingdom and its holy places." Unable to obtain a more decisive ruling from its own 'ulama, and constantly searching for wider approbation, the Saudi leadership turned to a leading Egyptian Islamic personality, Shaykh Muhammad

Mitwalli Sha'rawi. Saudi television then broadcast a statement from Sha'rawi, who quoted several instances when the prophet Muhammad had sought and received the aid of non-Muslims.[7] Only Bin Baz's allegiance to the Saudi regime and his view that its rulers knew best had overcome his reluctance to authorize the introduction of unbelieving troops into Saudi Arabia. However, a group of younger, radical 'ulama, known as the "Awakening Shaykhs," rejected this decision.

The Awakening Shaykhs

For many radical Sunni fundamentalist shaykhs, the fatwa that allowed Christian troops into the kingdom crossed a red line. In their minds, it was unfathomable how a leading *'alim* (Islamic scholar) could issue a ruling so blatantly at odds with the *shari'a* (Islamic law).[8]

Two relatively young 'ulama, Shaykh Salman bin Fahd al-'Awda and Shaykh Safar bin 'Abd al-Rahman al-Hawali, who have become known as *shuyukh al-sahwa* (the Awakening Shaykhs), led the radical Sunni fundamentalist movement after the Iraqi invasion. The popularity of these shaykhs stemmed from their willingness to speak out clearly and without fear about social and political wrongs.[9] In the Saudi milieu, this candor was a refreshing change, and it spoke to the thousands of youths who questioned the deeds of the Al Sa'ud.

Al-Hawali, a member of the Ghamid tribe, was born in 1950 in the province of al-Baha, south of the Hijazi mountain city of Ta'if. He had a traditional tribal upbringing and completed his bachelor's degree at the Islamic University in Medina. He received a master's degree from Umm al-Qura University in Mecca in 1981 and a doctorate from the same institution in 1986, writing his thesis on *'ilmaniyya* (secularism). He later taught at Umm al-Qura University in the Department of Theology (*'aqida*) and was later chair of that department. During the 1980s, al-Hawali became known for his lectures on Islamic theology and his defense of it against foreign ideologies. Just prior to the Iraqi invasion of Kuwait, he delivered several lectures on the fall of communism and the rise of Islamic fundamentalism as its replacement.[10]

Al-Hawali's most famous work is *Kissinger's Promise*, a book that claims to analyze Western designs on the oil resources of the Persian Gulf countries. The cover contains a map of the Arabian Peninsula with the flags of the United States, France, Britain, and other Western countries around it, and the volume ends with an appeal to his fellow Saudis:

> The Crusader [that is, Western and Christian] invasion of the Arabian Peninsula has already undermined the honor . . . of every Muslim. It will not be long until your blood is shed with impunity or you declare your abandonment of your belief in God.[11]

Al-Hawali's statements show evidence of a "Saudi" statist or nationalist perspective—Saudi nationalism dressed in Islamic clothes. Al-Hawali's supporters published and distributed many of his lectures on audiocassette.

Al-'Awda, a member of the Banu Khalid tribe, was born in 1955 in the village of al-Basr, just south of the city of Burayda in the province of Qasim in central Arabia. His family moved to Burayda while he was still in elementary school, and he completed high school there. He began his undergraduate studies in the Faculty of Arabic Language at Imam Muhammad bin Sa'ud Islamic University in Riyadh, but after two years he transferred to the Faculty of Shari'a, where he finished his studies. He received a master's degree from the Faculty of Shari'a and the Fundamentals of Religion (*usul al-din*) at the Qasim branch of the same university, where he also taught. He was fired from this post in July 1993 but remained a doctoral candidate there. He has written about ten books and recorded more than 500 audiocassette tapes.[12]

The popularity of these shaykhs reached its peak with the Gulf crisis and, according to sympathetic sources, was given further impetus by "the arrival of American troops in the *bilad al-haramayn* [land of the two holy shrines, Mecca and Medina]." According to the same sources, the two provided guidance and analysis to a frightened and bewildered Saudi public.[13]

After Saddam Husayn's August 1990 invasion of Kuwait,

the first sign of dissent in Saudi Arabia came from al-Hawali the following month. Addressing a large gathering at a mosque in northern Riyadh, al-Hawali said the real danger stemmed not from the secular Iraqi Ba'th party, as other preachers had claimed, but rather from the secular Syrian Ba'th, which had killed tens of thousands of its own Muslim citizens in Hama in 1982. The Syrian Ba'th was allied with the Saudi government in the coalition against Iraq. He castigated the government for its initial news blackout of the Iraqi invasion of Kuwait and for inviting non-Muslim troops to defend the country. Muslims, he said, should not join with infidels to fight other Muslims. According to al-Hawali, the serious threat was the United States, which was using the Iraqi invasion of Kuwait as a pretext to control the oil resources of the Persian Gulf: "It is not the world against Iraq," al-Hawali said. "It is the West against Islam. . . . [I]f Iraq has occupied Kuwait, then America has occupied Saudi Arabia. The real enemy is not Iraq. It is the West. . . . While Iraq was the enemy of the hour, America and the West were the enemies of Judgment Day." Saudis were not accustomed to hearing someone speak so clearly and forthrightly. A recording of al-Hawali's talk was made, and several million copies were distributed in the kingdom and overseas.[14]

Al-'Awda spoke a few days later, and his lecture was also recorded and widely distributed. Entitled *Suqut al-Duwal* (The Fall of States), al-'Awda's talk analyzed the collapse of states throughout history, and he said the Americans were coming to harvest the failure of the Saudi state that believed more in President George Bush than in God. As the copies of these two lectures were disseminated, the popularity of these two shaykhs grew.[15]

The presence of U.S. troops was probably responsible for the emboldening of the more secular and westernized elements of the population. The radical fundamentalists believed that the *'ilmaniyyin* (secularists) were collaborating with U.S. efforts to subvert Saudi society and put an end to the rule of religion.[16] On November 6, 1990, an unusual event occurred in Riyadh as seventy women dismissed their drivers and began driving around the city on their own. Although these women possessed licenses—they had all received driver's licenses in the United States or Europe—women are not allowed to drive in Saudi Arabia. The challenge to the Saudi status quo was even more serious as it took place in Najd, the Wahhabi heartland, not the more cosmopolitan Hijaz.[17] The radical fundamentalists perceived the women's actions as directly related to the U.S. troop presence, as female American soldiers were seen driving trucks around Riyadh—while wearing short pants, the radicals claimed. The Sunni radicals also believed that the emir of Riyadh, Salman bin 'Abd al-'Aziz, secretly supported the Saudi women's demonstration. Sunni fundamentalists were outraged, and hundreds of people signed petitions demanding that the offenders be punished or put to death. The regime was forced to act, outlawing such demonstrations and firing all of the women from their jobs. Additionally, Bin Baz issued a fatwa affirming the illegality of Saudi women driving.[18]

The government-sponsored crackdown on the women drivers and King Fahd's announcement in early November 1990 that he planned to initiate political reforms, including the creation of a *majlis al-shura* (consultative council),[19] was likely the immediate impetus for a petition submitted to the government in December 1990 by a group of forty-three liberal–modernist Saudis—businessmen and intellectuals, including former cabinet minister Muhammad 'Abduh Yamani. The signatories were keen to demonstrate their loyalty to the king, to "the present system of government, and to preserving the cherished royal family," but they proposed ten reforms. These proposals included the demand for a more open *ifta* (the process of rendering religious decisions) in which all Saudis could debate religious rulings; a basic law of government; formation of a consultative council with no demand that it be elected; reinstatement of elections for municipal councils; modernization of the judicial system; implementation of equal rights, regardless of ethnic, tribal, sectarian, or social origins; a free media; reform of the religious police; a greater public role for women in society; and educational reform.[20]

This petition alarmed al-'Awda, al-Hawali, and their radical Sunni fundamentalist followers, as it called into question the role of the 'ulama in ifta and attacked another of their centers of power, the religious police. This petition, combined with the demonstration of women drivers, moved the radical Sunni fundamentalists to take a drastic step of their own.

The Letter of Demands

The first organized radical fundamentalist response to the new situation in the country appeared in May 1991: a petition entitled *khitab al-matalib* (Letter of Demands), reflecting its simple but stark nature. After being widely circulated in mosques, it was handed to King Fahd in mid-May. The petition called for the establishment of a consultative council independent of any governmental influence; the repeal of all laws and regulations not conforming to the shari'a, as decided by competent committees; and the requirement that all government officials be moral and in no way corrupt. Justice, said the petitioners, must be applied fairly to all sectors of the population without favoritism. Public wealth must be distributed equally, with fees reduced and monopolies eliminated. Banks must be cleansed of usury. For national defense, a strong army was necessary, tasked only with protecting the country and the holy sites and supplied with arms from any source, with priority given to the development of a local arms industry. The news media, insisted the petition, must serve Islam and express the morals of society through the spread of awareness by constructive criticism and truthful reporting, within the confines of the shari'a. Foreign policy must be based on the national interest without relying on alliances not sanctioned by the shari'a, and it must embrace Islamic causes. Embassies must be reformed to reflect the Islamic nature of the country. Islamic religious institutions, particularly those related to furthering Islam, must be strengthened. Judicial institutions must be unified and allowed to operate independently. The rights of individuals must be guaranteed, in accordance with accepted religious safeguards.[21]

This document represented the first organized attempt by not only the radical 'ulama but also some establishment 'ulama to increase the power of religious figures in political decision making and to reject the government's increased marginalization of the 'ulama. The signatories wanted a voice in foreign policy, control of the media, an increased role in the judiciary, and more resources to spread their message. It was as if they desired to turn the clock back to the time of the Ikhwan, when the 'ulama had more influence and when, they believed, policymakers created public policy through the prism of furthering Islam. The published version of the petition contained fifty-two signatures. According to the opposition, a total of more than four hundred were eventually submitted. Among the signatories were the two shaykhs, as well as 'A'id al-Qarni, 'Awad al-Qarni, Nasir al-'Umar, and 'Abdallah bin al-Jibrin.[22]

It has been widely but erroneously assumed that Bin Baz and Shaykh Muhammad al-Salih al-'Uthaymin, a senior 'alim and Saudi Arabia's most prolific writer on religious issues, also signed this letter.[23] Bin Baz and al-'Uthaymin did send secret letters to the king supporting the petition and suggesting that he convene the Council of Senior 'Ulama to discuss the implementation of the reforms. They took this action in the tradition of presenting *nasiha* (advice) to the ruler in private concerning how best to govern according to Islamic law.[24]

For the Saudi government, the publication of the Letter of Demands was the last straw. Not only had the petition publicized matters the government preferred to keep under wraps, but it also demonstrated the government's lack of awareness of the large-scale organizing that had been occurring. According to opposition sources, the approximately four hundred 'ulama, judges, preachers, and university professors who signed the letter were individually interrogated by the security forces and forbidden to travel and lecture. Some were imprisoned but, following demonstrations in Najd and 'Asir, they were soon released.[25]

Shortly afterward, the petition's original signatories submitted another letter elaborating on the various points raised.

They stated that Bin Baz had asked them to issue these clarifications for submission to the Council of Senior 'Ulama. In
this document, which was much more harsh in its language,
the self-proclaimed reformers stated they had not wished the
earlier letter to be made public. They stated that the consultative council announced by King Fahd in November 1990
should be entirely independent and not a *suwari* (sham) council, as was the case in other countries. The clarifications also
included a list of laws, rules, and regulations adopted by the
government that conflicted with the shari'a, in part because
secular laymen unschooled in the Islamic sciences had drafted
them. The reformers attacked favoritism, nepotism, and corruption. The media was an abomination, carrying destructive
ideas, photographs of unveiled women, and sexual innu-
endo—accusations the signatories directed at the government
as the overseer of all media. Video stores abounded, the new
letter stated, selling pornography of the worst kind. The radicals paid particular attention to the lack of proper funding
for religious institutions, which had not benefited from the
oil boom. "Even more saddening," they stressed, "is that
allocations for one soccer team—for equipment, training,
management, and salaries—exceed the total expenditure on
all [religious] institutions." Evidence of the lack of individual
rights, they complained, was manifest in the harassment of
most of the signatories of the original petition, even though
they were only exercising their shari'a-sanctioned duty to
present nasiha to the ruler.[26]

Such discourse demonstrated that these religious men increasingly believed themselves to be outsiders. Proper
government, they demanded, involved the incorporation of
the 'ulama into all spheres of the administration. If the 'ulama
were allowed to manage the issues they had raised in the Letter of Demands and in the second explanatory letter, they
claimed that they would do so properly and fairly, for they
acted according to the shari'a, which by its very nature guaranteed such things.

Given the arrests and harassment, the government sorely
needed the establishment 'ulama to intervene on its side at

this crucial juncture. On June 3, 1991, the government prevailed upon the top 'ulama to issue a condemnation of the Letter of Demands. Their response came from both the Higher Judicial Council, a body within the Ministry of Justice, and the Council of Senior 'Ulama. The main point of the two councils' missives was that, while counsel by 'ulama was allowed, it should not be made public. Some observers viewed the language as an apology of sorts, because people like Bin Baz and al-'Uthaymin had privately associated themselves with the Letter of Demands.[27] Apparently, although the establishment 'ulama shared much of the radical fundamentalist agenda, they were uncomfortable with the radicals' public discussion of such matters. The event also demonstrated that the Saudi government could call on the establishment 'ulama for support if it pressed forcefully enough. The regime was thus successful in exploiting differences between the establishment 'ulama and the radicals, particularly over the form that criticism and advice should take.

Despite the regime's success, support for the agenda of the radical 'ulama did not diminish. Al-Hawali and al-'Awda grew more audacious in their attacks on the regime in the latter half of 1991, and their cassettes circulated widely. The establishment 'ulama upbraided them for their *khuruj* (deviation) from what the establishment believed to be the correct Islamic path.

While one group of radicals submitted the letter of clarification, another group decided to distribute two tapes narrated by an anonymous reader. The first tape was distributed in August 1991, and most copies bore the title "Supergun," employing the metaphor of a powerful weapon developed by Iraqi president Saddam Husayn to show the magnitude of the challenge to the regime. The preacher on the tape stressed that no allegiance is owed to princes unless they follow the shari'a. "The personal behavior of some of our rulers is so scandalous that it is the subject of books and articles abroad which damage our reputation," cried the speaker.[28]

The second tape was widely distributed in September 1991 and, according to the opposition, it had a great influence. Both tapes examined and criticized a wide range of Saudi domestic and foreign policies, basing their arguments on Islamic sources. A two-year-old tape by 'A'id al-Qarni also continued to enjoy great popularity during this time. Calling his tape "America as I Saw It," al-Qarni railed against the United States as a "nation of beasts who fornicate and eat rotten food." Furthermore, al-Qarni added, in America men marry men, women have children out of wedlock, and parents are abandoned in their old age, all leading to the decline of the United States.[29] Of course, the fact that the "Islamic" government of the Al Sa'ud had invited U.S. troops to the land of Mecca and Medina was not lost on al-Qarni's listeners.

In December 1991 the radical fundamentalists attacked two targets of particular political sensitivity: the female education system in Saudi Arabia and the Saudi Women's Renaissance Association. The establishment 'ulama controlled the former, but the radicals still attacked the women educators as whores. The latter included many prominent Saudi women, including members of the royal family. Despite these attacks, however, or perhaps because of the extreme nature of them, the majority of conservative Saudis continued to follow the regime and the establishment 'ulama. Bin Baz at this time rejected the "recording of poisonous allegations on cassettes and their distribution." He further berated the radicals for spreading "lies and conspiracies against Islam and Muslims." While speaking in a mosque, Prince Turki Al Faysal, head of the intelligence services, condemned the militants as extremists, saying they had slandered the royal family. He demanded that they either prove their claims or face the consequences.[30]

Saudi support for the Arab–Israeli peace process that had begun in Madrid in October 1991 led to further radical opposition. In January 1992, the preacher of the King Sa'ud University mosque was fired for refusing to endorse the Saudi-supported peace talks. This lack of endorsement was a sore spot for the regime. Members of the faculty protested the preacher's firing and met with Bin Baz. They eventually formed a committee, which later took the name of the University Committee for Reform and Advice. Bin Baz advised them to prepare a comprehensive document—a memorandum—covering all their grievances. The committee then sought advice from al-Hawali, al-'Awda, and other radical fundamentalist leaders who had signed the Letter of Demands.[31]

By January 1992, news of the Saudi government's response to the radical fundamentalists' activities had begun to spread. That month, the Western and foreign Arabic-language media reported that mosque preachers and imams had been detained for criticizing the government's support of direct Arab–Israeli peace talks. King Fahd hinted only that "certain forms of behavior" would be dealt with "if matters go too far."[32] Gen. 'Abdallah bin 'Abd al-Rahman Al al-Shaykh, the Saudi director of public security, was more explicit—by Saudi standards: The government, he said, would vigorously apply the law to groups of "sick-minded people" who had committed "recent crimes."[33] The government vigorously denied the reports, however, and the Saudi Press Agency quoted a "responsible source" saying that, with respect to reports of "the existence of arrests and differences of opinion in the Kingdom of Saudi Arabia, we wish to reiterate that all these reports are totally baseless and have no shred of truth."[34]

With the multilateral component of the Arab–Israeli peace talks scheduled to commence—with Saudi participation—in Moscow later that month, the Saudi regime acted against several radical fundamentalist 'ulama, arresting some and removing others from their posts.[35] Among them were some who had spoken out against Saudi support for the peace talks, whether from the pulpit or through cassette tapes.[36] The radical fundamentalists, some of whom were part of a loosely organized group called *al-sahwa al-Islamiyya* (Islamic Awakening)—a term used to connote the revivalist trend in the country—had reportedly been organizing a demonstration with more than a thousand marchers to protest the regime's participation in the peace talks.[37] Al-Hawali in particular was outspoken against the peace talks. All they would lead to, he argued, was the strengthening of the Jews at the expense of the Muslims. Al-Hawali concluded that God had promised the Jews only suffering until the end of days. "Hitler," he

added, "was a part of this promise, and the [Palestine] liberation and *jihad* movements are a part of this promise as well."[38]

One of the most serious developments within the Saudi
radical fundamentalist movement was the call for a charge of
takfir against the Saudi state.[39] Takfir, or pronouncing one's
unbelief, was the gravest of charges that could be leveled at
any Muslim—let alone against a regime that had an Islamic
raison d'être—because it was a proclamation of unbelief, not
merely moral failings. Many senior establishment 'ulama may
have agreed with this charge, as with other charges leveled by
the radicals, but because of their position close to the center
of power, they were reluctant to express themselves. Despite
the seriousness of the situation, however, it was not unique in
Saudi history. Takfir had been pronounced against the Saudi
leadership during the Ikhwan rebellion of 1927-1930 and
again during the attack by Juhayman al-'Utaybi in 1979. On
both occasions, the senior establishment 'ulama had come
to the defense of the ruling family, but this time the senior
'ulama were silent.

The Memorandum of Exhortation

In the summer of 1992, the King Sa'ud University Committee for Reform and Advice organized the writing of a detailed
memorandum of grievances and submitted it to Bin Baz, as
he had suggested. A cover letter asked him to review it and
submit it to King Fahd. Instead, the memorandum was leaked
to the Paris-based daily, *al-Muharrir*.[40] Entitled *mudhakkirat
al-nasiha* (The Memorandum of Exhortation),[41] it was signed
by more than one hundred 'ulama and university professors.

Al-Hawali, al-'Awda, 'Abdallah bin al-Jibrin, and 'Abdallah
al-Jalali wrote the introduction to the memorandum.[42] The
document criticized the government for its arrest of religious
figures and adopted a more strident tone than the 1991 petition. Covering several areas, the memorandum condemned
the government for providing aid to non-Islamic governments
such as Jordan, Algeria, Egypt, Syria, and Russia. It echoed
previous concerns about an over-financed military that did
not meet expectations and argued instead for compulsory

military service and the creation of a reserve corps. The petitioners disparaged the government for not adequately helping the Muslims in Bosnia. They said the government should increase religious media programming (already well over 50 percent of the broadcasts) and not show programs glorifying "decadent Western lifestyles." Again bristling at the monopoly on religion granted to the establishment 'ulama, the radical fundamentalists demanded total freedom of expression without the need to seek approval from the establishment 'ulama. They also wanted to establish their own press and broadcast companies to be overseen by a supreme consultative council of 'ulama, presumably of their own ilk.[43]

In other words, they sought both to remove the government and its official 'ulama from their role as the sole arbiters of Islam in the state and to return religion to the more decentralized nature it enjoyed before Ibn Sa'ud and before Faysal inaugurated his reforms. Most apparent from the language used in the memorandum was that the new statutes announce by King Fahd in March 1992 (see chapter 7) had not daunted the radical fundamentalist opposition. This sent a clear message to the king that fighting the radicals would not be easy.

Yet, Fahd did fight back, enlisting the Council of Senior 'Ulama to counter the memorandum. In mid-September 1992, the council condemned the memorandum in a statement signed by Bin Baz and the council members, denying the published "false allegations" that Bin Baz had contributed to the memorandum. The council accused the petitioners of fostering dissent, creating and exaggerating the kingdom's shortcomings, and ignoring all the good work done by the state. The memorandum, wrote the establishment 'ulama, conflicted with the methods of providing religious advice consistent with Islam, and the people who signed the memorandum had "deviationist ideological links" engendering discord.[44]

Significantly, the notation that they were absent for medical reasons accompanied the signatures of seven of the council members. It later became evident that they had actually not attended the meeting called to discuss the petition, claiming ill health.[45] King Fahd believed they took this action because they refused to condemn the radicals' petition. It is most likely that they actually supported the petition, demonstrating that the king had serious problems even among the establishment 'ulama. In late November, the king called their bluff, appointing ten new 'ulama to the council and, a few days later, removing those seven "ill" 'ulama, since they claimed that they were too sick to carry out their duties.[46]

The "sick-out" of seven of the country's top clerics was a manifest demonstration of the inroads made by the radicals and their agenda. Apparently, several establishment 'ulama shared many of the same concerns as the radical fundamentalist 'ulama. The Saudis, however, denied in mid-December that rifts existed between the government and the senior 'ulama.[47]

After this incident, King Fahd spoke on national television, upbraiding the radical clerics for airing their grievances and the country's problems in public. He said increasing Islamic fundamentalism in other countries was not good for them or for Saudi Arabia. Adoption by the Saudi radical fundamentalists of the methods of communication used in other countries, such as cassettes and leaflets, did not further the interests of Saudi Arabia. Fahd believed the state's only purpose was serving Islam, which Saudi Arabia did; those who would thus oppose the policies of the state in the name of religion were wrong. The leaders were always willing, Fahd continued, to listen to legitimate verbal or written criticism. But the use of clubs or other forums, cassettes, and leaflets "for worldly purposes or for matters unrelated to [the] public interest" was harmful.

> I hope that efforts will be confined to giving advice for the sake of God. If, however, someone has things to say, then he can always come to those in charge and speak to them in any region, in any place. As advice[,] this is wanted and desired. What is not desired is to bring issues out into the open. As far as bringing issues out into the open is concerned, even though in the past we have turned a blind eye to it, naturally I want it to be understood clearly that

no blind eye will be turned to anything that causes damage first to the creed, second to the national interest, and
third to anything that changes the existing situation.[48]

Groups of radical fundamentalist 'ulama continued to meet,
desperate to find the most suitable way to protest the arrest
of their members who, they believed, were only carrying out
their duty as sanctioned by the shari'a. In December 1992,
the authorities arrested a prominent 'alim, Shaykh Ibrahim
al-Dibyan of Qasim, in a reportedly brutal manner. The 'ulama
convened a meeting at the home of Shaykh Hamad al-Sulayfih
to discuss the matter. Although some wanted to treat Shaykh
al-Dibyan arrest as an isolated case, a smaller group wanted
to use it as a launching point for an organization that would
champion the cause of those 'ulama who wished to criticize
the regime freely.[49] This group would, in the next year, form
the Committee for the Defense of Legitimate Rights
(CDLR).[50]

In 1993, two other incidents displayed the increasingly
common agenda of the radicals and the establishment. First,
in March, the pro-Iraqi, Paris-based weekly *al-Muharrir* published a fatwa by the establishment Shaykh 'Abdallah bin
al-Jibrin attacking *al-Sharq al-Awsat*, a major Saudi daily published abroad and, more important, owned by Prince Salman
bin 'Abd al-'Aziz, the governor of Riyadh, and his sons.[51]
Al-Jibrin castigated the Saudi paper for publishing news that
humiliated Muslims, as well as stories and photographs of in-
fidel actors and actresses; he forbade Muslims from
purchasing or distributing the paper. The fatwa reportedly
was widely distributed at King Sa'ud University.[52]

Second, Bin Baz issued *nasiha* (advice, but in this case
more of an admonition) against traveling overseas to study,
particularly in the summer. As the premier 'alim in the country, Bin Baz stressed that Muslims enjoy God's favor and,
therefore, draw the envy and hatred of non-Muslims, who try
to corrupt them. He attacked travel agencies that attempted
to draw young Saudis to Europe or the United States to study
English and perhaps stay with non-Muslim families, creating

the danger of attending parties with women. He said non-Muslims overseas would cause Muslims to doubt their faith, become lax in fulfilling their duties, develop hedonistic tendencies, and be dazzled by Western culture. "I therefore warn my Muslim brothers in Saudi Arabia and other lands against journeying to these countries," stressed Bin Baz. If they wanted to travel, he suggested they perform the *'umra* in Mecca or visit the prophet's mosque in Medina.[53] Many upper-class Saudis typically sent their children abroad to study, and the implications of Bin Baz's admonition were thus not lost on the elite and the ruling family: "Good" Muslims did not send their children abroad in the summer.

Notes

1. Joseph Kostiner, "Saudi Arabia," in Ami Ayalon, ed., *Middle East Contemporary Survey (MECS), 1991* (Boulder, Colo.: Westview, 1993), pp. 613–640.

2. On the concept of "cycle of crisis" and its role in the emergence of Islamic resurgency, see R. Hrair Dekmejian, "Islamic Revival: Catalysts, Categories, and Consequences," in Shireen Hunter, ed., *The Politics of Islamic Revival* (Bloomington: Indiana University Press, 1988), pp. 3-19.

3. See, for example, 'A'id bin 'Abdallah al-Qarni, *Qul Hadha Sabili* [Say: This is My Path] (Riyadh: Dar al-Watan lil-Nashr, n.d.), distributed by the Ministry of Labor and Public Works. Pamphlets by other leading radical fundamentalists, such as Salman bin Fahd al-'Awda and Nasir bin Sulayman al-'Umar were also distributed in the same manner.

4. See Movement for Islamic Reform in Arabia (MIRA), *History of Dissent: The Story of Islamic Dissent in Arabia,* chapter 1, "Al Saud, Islam, and the Reform Movement," online at http://www.miraserve.com/chap1.html.

5. Nawaf Obaid, "Improving U.S. Intelligence Analysis on the Saudi Decision-Making Process," John F. Kennedy School of Government, May 1, 1998; Obaid's paper is also discussed in *al-Quds al-'Arabi,* July 15, 1998, and *The Independent,* September 2, 1998.

6. The translated English text of the fatwa as reported by Radio Riyadh on August 13, 1990, is in "Ulema Council Supports Actions of King Fahd," FBIS-DR-90-157, August 14, 1990, p. 26; the original Arabic is in *'Ukaz,* August 14, 1990.

7. Jacob Goldberg, "Saudi Arabia," in Ami Ayalon, ed., *MECS 1990* (Boulder, Colo.: Westview, 1992) pp. 606–607; Riyadh TV, September 19, reported in "Scholar Justifies Non-Muslim Aid in Crisis," FBIS-DR-90-183, p. 18.

8. See MIRA, *History of Dissent*, chapter 3, "The Gulf Crisis and the Islamic Revival," online at http://www.miraserve.com/chap3.html.

9. Muhammad Al-Rifa'i, *Al-Mashru' al-Islahi fi al-Sa'udiyya: Qissat al-Hawali wal-'Awda* [The Reform Program in Saudi Arabia: The Story of al-Hawali and al-'Awda] (unpublished manuscript, 1995).

10. Al-Rifa'i, *Al-Mashru' al-Islahi fi al-Sa'udiyya*, pp. 16–17; al-*Majalla*, October 9–15, 1994.

11. Safar bin 'Abd Al-Rahman Al-Hawali, *Wa'd Kissinger: al-Ahdaf al-Amrikiyya fil-Khalij* [Kissinger's Promise: American Goals in the Gulf] (Dallas: Mu'assat al-Kitab al-Islami, n.d.), p. 158. The Council of Senior 'Ulama cited this book in their decision permitting the arrest of Hawali in September 1994. For a detailed description of the content of this book and an analysis of Hawali's thought, see Mamoun Fandy, "Safar Al-Hawali: Saudi Islamist or Saudi Nationalist?" *Islam and Christian–Muslim Relations* 9 (March 1998), pp. 5–21.

12. Al-Rifa'i, *Al-Mashru' al-Islahi fi al-Sa'udiyya*, pp. 17–18; "Salman bin Fahd Al-Auda: Short Biography," distributed by MSANEWS and in the author's possession.

13. Al-Rifa'i, *Al-Mashru' al-Islahi fi al-Sa'udiyya*, p. 18.

14. Peter Wilson and Douglas Graham, *Saudi Arabia: The Coming Storm* (Armonk, N.Y.: M.E. Sharpe, 1994), pp. 61–62; Al-Rifa'i, *Al-Mashru' al-Islahi fi al-Sa'udiyya*, pp. 11–14; MIRA, *History of Dissent*, chapter 3; Goldberg, "Saudi Arabia," p. 617.

15. Al-Rifa'i, *Al-Mashru' al-Islahi fi al-Sa'udiyya*, pp. 13–14; MIRA, *History of Dissent in Arabia*, chapter 3.

16. Al-Rifa'i, *Al-Mashru' al-Islahi fi al-Sa'udiyya*, p. 20.

17. On the driving demonstration, see Goldberg, "Saudi Arabia," pp. 621–623.

18. Al-Rifa'i, *Al-Mashru' al-Islahi fi al-Sa'udiyya*, p. 20–21; Goldberg, "Saudi Arabia," pp. 621-623.

19. Goldberg, "Saudi Arabia," pp. 619–620. Fahd had promised similar reforms a decade earlier, following disturbances in the Shi'i Eastern Province.

20. See Aziz Abu Hamad, "Empty Reforms: Saudi Arabia's New Basic Laws," *Middle East Watch* (a publication of Human Rights Watch), May 1992. See also Mordechai Abir, *Saudi Arabia: Government, Society, and the Gulf Crises* (London: Routledge, 1993), pp. 186–189.

21. Al-Rifa'i, *Al-Mashru' al-Islahi fi al-Sa'udiyya*, pp. 108–109; al-*Sha'b*, May 21, 1991 (full Arabic text).

22. Al-'Umar wrote a pamphlet on the heresy of the Shi'a, entitled "Ahwal al-Rafidha fi Bilad al-Tawhid" [The Status of the Renegades in the Country of Monotheism]. He was released from Saudi custody along with the Awakening Shaykhs in June 1999. Shaykh 'Abdallah bin al-Jibrin—a member of the General Presidency of *Ifta, Da'wa,* and *Irshad*, was noted for his fatwa asserting that Shi'is should be killed as heretics.

   R. Hrair Dekmejian has analyzed the social composition of this Islamist elite, based on those who signed the Letter of Demands and the September 1992 Memorandum of Exhortation (on this memorandum, see below). This elite was relatively homogenous, hailed mostly from Najd (63 percent of the signatories of the letter; 72 percent of the memorandum), and held academic or religious positions or both. About a dozen or so were already well-known critics of the regime. R. Hrair Dekmejian, "The Rise of Political Islam in Saudi Arabia," *Middle East Journal* 48 (autumn 1994), pp. 635–638.

23. See Abu Hamad. The reason for uncertainty is that the most widely published version, in the Egyptian newspaper *al-Sha'b* on May 21, 1991, and reprinted by al-Rifa'i, does not contain their signatures, only the addendum that Bin Baz added "on the basis of the Islamic shari'a" to one of the articles, that Al-'Uthaymin supported Bin Baz's amendment, and that the copy submitted to the king included it. Al-Rifa'i does not state that the two shaykhs had signed the petition, but rather that it bore their *tazkiyya* (approbation). Al-Rifa'i, *Al-Mashru' al-Islahi fi al-Sa'udiyya*, p. 60. Indeed, if they had signed the letter, they would not have had to send a separate letter of support. If they had signed it, it would have demonstrated an ever greater degree of penetration of radical ideas into the Islamic establishment.

24. The letters to Fahd are dated late April 1991. Al-Rifa'i, *Al-Mashru' al-Islahi fi al-Sa'udiyya*, pp. 101–115; *al-Jazira al-'Arabiyya*, September 1991, pp. 12–13.

25. *Al-Quds al-'Arabi*, August 1, 1991; Abir, *Saudi Arabia: Government, Society and the Gulf Crises*, p. 192.

26. Al-Rifa'i, *Al-Mashru' al-Islahi fi al-Sa'udiyya*, pp. 117–126; *al-Quds al-'Arabi*, August 1, 1991; and *al-Jazira al-'Arabiyya*, September 1991 (containing text of the explanatory letter).

27. Kostiner, "Saudi Arabia," p. 628; Abir, *Saudi Arabia: Government, Society and the Gulf Crises*, p. 192; Economist Intelligence Unit, *Country Report: Saudi Arabia*, no. 2 (1991).

28. *International Herald Tribune*, March 10, 1992.

29. See MIRA, *History of Dissent*, chapter 8, "'Supergun' in Riyadh," online at http://www.miraserve.com/chap8.html; see also *International Herald Tribune*, March 10, 1992.

30. Abir, *Saudi Arabia: Government, Society and the Gulf Crises*, pp. 194–198.

31. See MIRA, *History of Dissent*, chapter 9, "The Memorandum of Advice," online at http://www.miraserve.com/chap9.html.

32. See *al-Sharq al-Awsat*, January 28, in the daily report of the Foreign Broadcast Information Service Near East and South Asia Daily Report (FBIS-NES), January 31, 1992.

33. See *al-Sharq al-Awsat*, January 30, in "Public Security Director on 'Sick-Minded People,'" FBIS-NES-92-023, February 4, 1992, p. 25.

34. Saudi Press Agency (SPA), February 8, in "'Source' Says Reports 'Baseless'," FBIS-NES-92-027, February 10, 1992, p. 25. See also SPA, February 3, in "'Official Source' Denies Arrest, Dissent," FBIS-NES-92-032, February 18, 1992, p. 20.

35. See *al-Quds al-'Arabi*, January 11–12, 1992, in "Authorities Round Up Dissident Imams, Preachers," FBIS-NES-92-011, January 16, 1992, p. 24; *al-Quds al-'Arabi*, January 28, 1992, in "Judge Dismissed for Opposing U.S. Presence," FBIS-NES-92-032, February 4, 1992, p. 24; *al-Sha'b* (Cairo), February 4, 1992, in "Authorities Arrest 250 Preachers, Launch Manhunt," FBIS-NES-92-027, February 10, 1992, p. 25.

36. Agence France-Presse, January 29, 1992.

37. Youssef Ibrahim, "Saudi King Takes On Islamic Militants," *New York Times*, January 30, 1992, p. A3; *Christian Science Monitor*, March 16, 1992.

38. *Ha'aretz*, August 21, 1992 (quoting al-Hawali).

39. See *al-Safir*, March 3, 1992.

40. See MIRA, *History of Dissent*, chapter 10, "Reactions to the Memorandum," online at http://www.miraserve.com/chap10.html.

41. Such exhortations, or advice, were an honored tradition in Saudi Arabia, dating back to the first Saudi state in the mid-eighteenth century, and were based on the doctrine of the Hanbali jurist Ibn Taymiyya, whose famous treatise *al-Siyasa al-Shar'iyya* [The Islamic Polity] had provided the conceptual framework for Muhammad bin 'Abd al-Wahhab. Ibn Taymiyya had written that qualified individuals had the right and duty to offer *nasiha* (exhortation). M.J. Crawford, "Civil War, Foreign Intervention, and the Question of Legitimacy: A Nineteenth Century Sa'udi Qadi's Dilemma," *International Journal of Middle Eastern Studies* 14 (1982), pp. 227–248.

42. Al-Rifa'i, *Al-Mashru' al-Islahi fi al-Sa'udiyya*, p. 64; *al-Muharrir*, September 14, 1992.

43. The memorandum has been published in various forms. See, for example, *al-Wa'y*, January 1993. Its contents are summarized in English in MIRA, *History of Dissent*, chapter 10. See also Youssef M. Ibrahim, "Saudi Clergymen Seek Tighter Islamic Rule," *New York Times*, October 8, 1992, p. A6; *Washington Post*, December 18, 1992.

44. See *al-Jazira*, September 18, 1991. The full text of the statement can be found in Al-Rifa'i, *Al-Mashru' al-Islahi fi al-Sa'udiyya*, pp. 128–129; see also *al-Muharrir*, September 14, 1992.

45. *Sunday Times*, December 13, 1992.

46. Riyadh TV, November 30, 1992, in "King Fahd Appoints 10 to Senior Ulema Body," FBIS-NES-92-231 , December 1, 1992, p. 20.

47. *'Ukaz*, September 19, 1992.

48. Riyadh TV, December 20, 1992, in "King Fahd Addresses Citizens on Islam, Future," FBIS-NES-92-245, December 21, 1992, p. 26; *al-Sharq al-Awsat*, December 22, 1992.

49. See MIRA, *History of Dissent*, chapter 11, "The Committee for the Defence of Legitimate Rights," online at http://www.miraserve.com/chap11.html.

50. See Agence France-Presse, reporting on the connection between the arrest of Dibyan and the formation of the CDLR, on May 9, 1993, in "Human Rights Group to Fight 'Oppression, Injustice,'" FBIS-NES-93-083, May 11, 1993, p. 24.

51. Bin al-Jibrin was well-known for his 1991 fatwa proclaiming the Shi'a apostates and calling for their death. See *al-Jazira al-'Arabiyya*, December 1991.

52. See *al-Muharrir*, March 29, 1993.

53. See *al-Hayat* (London), July 14, 1993. The *'umra* is the non-obligatory visitation to the Ka'ba that a Muslim may undertake outside of the hajj season.

Chapter 4

Institutionalizing the Radical Fundamentalist Opposition: The Founding of the CDLR

The most widely publicized and daring opposition activity occurred on May 3, 1993, when six radical fundamentalists publicly declared the establishment of the Committee for the Defense of Legitimate Rights (CDLR).[1]

Four of the six founders of the committee had signed the "Memorandum of Exhortation" submitted to King Fahd in 1992, one indication of the continuation and emboldening of the radical Sunni fundamentalist movement in Saudi Arabia. The four were Shaykh Dr. 'Abdallah bin Hamud al-Tuwayjri, chairman of the Department of Sunna at Imam Muhammad bin Sa'ud Islamic University, Riyadh, and a retired *qadi* (Islamic judge); Sulayman bin Ibrahim al-Rushudi, attorney; Shaykh 'Abdallah bin Sulayman al-Mas'ari, attorney, former head of the Board of Grievances, and associate of the kingdom's leading cleric, Shaykh 'Abd al-'Aziz bin Baz; and Shaykh Dr. 'Abdallah bin 'Abd al-Rahman bin al-Jibrin, a senior *'alim* (religious leader).

The other two CDLR founders were Hamad al-Sulayfih, a senior Ministry of Education official; and Dr. 'Abdallah al-Hamid, poet and professor of religion at Imam Muhammad Ibn Sa'ud Islamic University. 'Abdallah al-Mas'ari's son, Muhammad, a lecturer in physics at King Sa'ud University, also signed the "Memorandum of Exhortation" and was associated with the CDLR, but he did not sign the committee's founding document.[2] These activists openly courted the Western media by fax and met with officials of the U.S. Embassy in Riyadh.[3]

49

On May 6, 'Abdallah al-Mas'ari spoke with the British Broadcasting Corporation (BBC), live from Riyadh, assisted by his son Muhammad, who speaks fluent English.[4] In his interview with the BBC, al-Mas'ari indicated that the timing of the group's appearance was in part because of the multiparty elections held in Yemen on April 27. He said, "I am convinced that the Saudi society has more educated people, has [a] more middle-class structure which is more suitable for elections [than in Yemen], that it should be here successful or even more." At the prompting of the BBC correspondent, al-Mas'ari stressed that the CDLR was interested in human rights and due process, which the reporter interpreted naïvely as "a sort of general modernization of what we would know in the West as civic society." Al-Mas'ari maintained that the committee would be able to achieve much because it was speaking within an Islamic discourse and enjoyed the support and protection of the *'ulama* (religious leaders).[5]

The CDLR's turn to the West and portrayal of itself as a human rights organization was Muhammad al-Mas'ari's doing. He differed from the "Awakening Shaykhs" mentioned in chapter 3—Safar bin 'Abd al-Rahman al-Hawali and Salman bin Fahd al-'Awda—in that he was educated in the West and fluent in English. He was comfortable in the Western idiom, and unlike the Awakening Shaykhs, he "repackaged" the radical fundamentalist message for a Western audience. In doing so, he was similar to Sudan's Hasan al-Turabi and Tunisia's Rashid al-Ghannushi.[6]

The CDLR's founding announcement, entitled *al-Islah* (reform), was an appeal to "eliminate injustice and support the oppressed . . . and defend the rights prescribed by the *shari'a* [Islamic law]." The document also called for an end to travel bans and torture, the separation of political and legislative authorities, and a review of existing laws to ensure that they conformed with Islamic law.[7] In short, the CDLR members were echoing a call issued by Islamists in other countries for more participation and for greater accountability of public officials—demands based, they argued, on Islamic principles. Furthermore, as senior men of religion, they established themselves as a clearinghouse for complaints of mistreatment by the authorities, a role they believed was proper under the shari‘a.

Saudi authorities were quick to crush the CDLR. Prince Salman, the governor of Riyadh, summoned the group to a meeting on May 8 and informed its members that they had violated the norms of the kingdom.[8] A few days later, the Council of Senior ‘Ulama issued a statement condemning the CDLR as illegal "because the Kingdom of Saudi Arabia, thanks to God, rules by God's law, and the *shar‘i* [Islamic legal] courts are spread all over the country and no one is prevented from taking his grievances to the competent authorities. . . ."[9] The next day, the regime fired the CDLR activists from their jobs and closed down the offices of the attorneys. The activists were arrested soon afterward.[10]

The CDLR's spokesman, Muhammad al-Mas‘ari, who had readily engaged the Western media in the past, soon began to avoid their questions because of pressure from the regime. Nevertheless, the CDLR continued to issue written statements. In a revealing document published in June 1993, the CDLR described its self-perceived function and responded to the government's attacks. "The committee members are working and struggling for shar‘i goals" and are certain of the legitimacy of their work, it stated. The statement continued that the shari‘a forbids punishment of an ‘alim who has reached a decision on a religious question, relying on religious sources, simply because the government disagrees with him. If the authorities thought the committee contradicted Islamic law, then they would have to prove that assertion under the shari‘a. The members stressed that the CDLR was not a political party, a judicial authority, or an alternative to existing bodies.[11]

The CDLR: Opposition in Exile

Muhammad al-Mas‘ari was released in November 1993, went underground, passed through Yemen, and finally surfaced in London in April 1994, where he established the CDLR headquarters. Educated in the West and married to an American, al-Mas'ari quickly realized the importance of distributing his message to the widest possible audience in the West as well as within Saudi Arabia. To this end, he used electronic mail to publish communiqués and his bulletin, the *CDLR Monitor*, over the Internet; to send messages to Saudi Arabia, fax machines were the most frequently used means of communication. For sympathizers inside the kingdom, al-Mas'ari published AT&T and MCI calling-card numbers with precise instructions on dialing a number in the United States to reach the CDLR toll-free while avoiding Saudi intelligence. Al-Mas'ari's use of telecommunications technology helped to disseminate the CDLR's message and allowed unprecedented penetration of Saudi Arabia and distribution abroad. The publicity the CDLR received in its first year granted the organization a position of primacy as the voice not only of various trends in Saudi Islamism, but also of tribal groups and liberal modernists who were fearful of speaking out yet supportive of some aspects of the CDLR's political message.

Al-Mas'ari spent his first few months in London publicizing appeals on behalf of radical fundamentalists and of family members who had been arrested in the wake of his flight. Those arrested included several university professors, as well as al-Mas'ari's young son, his brother, two brothers-in-law, and other family members. In all, the CDLR reported the arrests of large numbers of sympathizers, many from Qasim.[12] These initial activities meshed well with the CDLR's attempt to portray itself as a human rights organization.

Britain, with its long tradition of support for the Al Sa'ud, rejected al-Mas'ari's application for political asylum in November 1994, a decision that he appealed.[13] In January 1996, the British authorities ordered the deportation of al-Mas'ari to the Caribbean island of Dominica. "British interests as a whole do require his removal," said Home Office Minister Ann Widdencombe. "We have enormous export considerations."[14] But in March, an immigration appeals judge ordered the government to reconsider al-Mas'ari's request for political asylum.[15] In April, having given up hope of quickly deporting him, the government decided to allow him to stay in Britain for four years, in an apparent compromise between expelling him and granting him full asylum.[16] As of this writing, in September 2000, he remains in Britain.

In interviews to the general press and in the *CDLR Monitor* and its Arabic-language counterpart *al-Huquq*, the organization concentrated on what it saw as the corruption and favoritism of the Saudi royal family at the expense of the public purse.[17] For example, it noted that the telecommunications firm Ericsson had submitted a proposal priced at less than half that of an AT&T bid for a massive Saudi telecommunications project, and that the conditions of the tender handed to Ericsson were different from—and more extensive than—those delivered to AT&T. Nevertheless, the AT&T bid was accepted. "It remains to be noted," commented *al-Huquq* dryly, "that 'Abd Al-Aziz bin Fahd [King Fahd's son] is the representative of that company [AT&T]."[18] Highlighting numerous examples of the kingdom's water and electricity shortages and the regime's failures to pay workers and contractors,[19] the CDLR also drew attention to royal family scandals. Each of Ibn Saud's sons, for example, was reportedly given a payment of 100 million Saudi riyals (about $26.66 million) in April 1994.[20] The CDLR's intention for publishing these allegations was to expose the suffering of the common people while the royal family squandered the nation's wealth.

Although not directly endorsing violence and sometimes actually disavowing it,[21] the CDLR warned that violence might result if the regime continued to oppress opposition activists. It took credit for preventing "radical discourses" and claimed to be "the only viable alternative to violent and chaotic methods, which were imminent due to the growth of corruption, oppression, and human rights violations." Nonetheless, the organization publicized calls to violence by others. It quoted some "zealous youths" who had promised to kill five members of the ruling family for each CDLR member harmed. "We at CDLR don't believe that things will reach such a stage and [therefore] call for restraint." Most significantly, the CDLR was the first group to publish the announcement of an organization called the *Kata'ib al-Iman* (Battalions of Faith), which threatened violence in Saudi Arabia following the Burayda arrests in September 1994 (see below). "CDLR warns that if such a trend starts in the kingdom, it is going to be much more [bloody] than [in] Egypt or Algeria. People are heavily armed and there is no lack of devotion among thousands of militant men."[22]

The CDLR's public image was that of a sophisticated, enlightened group encouraging debate in the kingdom. It sought "to destroy the unfounded belief that any type of organization or gathering is *haram* [forbidden]," and it perceived itself as entirely committed to the Qur'an and the Sunna and as an "integral part of the *sahwa* [awakening] in the kingdom."[23] The CDLR, however, clearly stated that Saudi Arabia "was a totalitarian state, the very antithesis of the will of the people." It was "most certainly not a people-centered society[,] as in the case of the Scandinavian social democracies."[24] But it was vague about what type of government it desired in Saudi Arabia. Muhammad al-Mas'ari said the new Saudi Arabia "will be an Islamic state, but not a theocratic one. There is a model—the Caliphate after the Prophet."[25]

The CDLR was often termed a "human rights organization" in the Western press, an image al-Mas'ari wished to project to gain the support of Western countries that might pressure Saudi Arabia. Indeed, some of the CDLR's demands sounded quite attractive to Western ears: more participation in decision making, free discussion, a free press, and so forth. Although the CDLR's demands included human rights, freedom of expression, and opposition to authoritarianism, however, these calls were made not out of a commitment to democratic values, but because the CDLR believed them to be necessary so their real demands would be met: The organization wanted the Saudi regime to open up da'wa activities to those who did not follow the establishment 'ulama; to apply Islamic law more strictly, and to adopt "Islamic" views on foreign policy.

The CDLR attacked the very foundation of the Saudi system by calling into question the age-old alliance between the 'ulama and the *umara* (princes). For the CDLR, the 'ulama only covered up the misdeeds of the royal family, the Al Saʻud. The CDLR claimed that the umara feigned respect for scholars; referring to the establishment ʻulama, the CDLR wrote: "Some of their paid accomplices . . . helped to project a highly favorable image of the miscreant [Al Saʻud] while suppressing the squalid reality."[26] The CDLR wrote that, when the founder of the kingdom, Ibn Saʻud, was unable to enlist the scholars' support, he enforced their silence. It declared that King Fahd, in turn, had "antagonized the most credible of the scholars, and the ones with the most influence in society." He had recklessly appropriated the role of head ʻalim and *mufti* (an issuer of religious decisions) by creating the Supreme Council for Islamic Affairs and packing it with hand-picked members.[27] In the view of the CDLR, Fahd had circumvented the legitimate scholars. The CDLR viewed the creation of the council as an attempt to hijack Islamic legitimacy and to consolidate "Islam according to Al Saʻud." It protested the choice of Defense Minister Prince Sultan bin ʻAbd al-ʻAziz to head the council because, the CDLR claimed, he was "renowned for his hatred and abuse of preachers and scholars."[28]

At the same time as the CDLR was being established, the Saudi government was preparing its case against the Awakening Shaykhs, al-Hawali and al-ʻAwda. Al-Hawali was asked to remain in the country and to desist from his activities. When he refused to sign any documents agreeing to these requests, the king instructed the Council of Senior ʻUlama in September 1993 to study his writings and taped lectures, as well as those of al-ʻAwda. The council determined that the two shaykhs had made mistakes and should be invited to retract them. If they refused, they should be forbidden to lecture and to record cassettes. They were called to a meeting at the Interior Ministry in Jeddah later that month, where they met with an official of the Ministry of the Interior and with the director of *al-Mabahith* (Intelligence). The ministry official read a series of charges, asking the two shaykhs to admit in writing to their wrongdoing and to desist from their activities. They refused.[29]

The Burayda Demonstration and
the Arrest of the Awakening Shaykhs

Radical Sunni fundamentalist activity increased during the summer of 1994, and radical fundamentalist leaders openly criticized anything reflecting positively on the regime. For example, the Saudi regime and many of its citizens were proud of the national team's participation in the World Cup soccer games in the United States. The games were a royal event, attended by several princes as well as thousands of Saudi students in the United States. King Fahd even telephoned the coach on the eve of their game against Belgium.[30] In the frenzy following the team's 1-0 victory in that game, which put it in the final sixteen, Saudi officials announced that each player would receive $267,000 as a bonus. The radical fundamentalists, however, rejected the entire event. Al-'Awda appealed to Saudis at U.S. universities to ignore the "football farce." Not only was it a waste of money, he said, but attending the matches contradicted the religious way of life and tempted one to drink, take drugs, and engage in forbidden relations. Instead, he argued, Saudi students in the United States should engage in Islamic missionizing and concentrate on defeating the enemies of Islam.[31]

Al-'Awda and al-Hawali, as well as several other scholars and founding members of the CDLR, issued a statement condemning the Saudi regime's support of southern Yemen in the Yemeni civil war, which had started in early May 1994. They referred to "the crimes of the communists in the south [who] . . . killed their shaykhs and 'ulama," and they beseeched God to "make the truth (*al-haqq*) and its people victorious" and to "defeat polytheism (*al-shirk*) and its people."[32] *Shirk* was the polar opposite of the Wahhabi doctrine of *tawhid* (unity of God); such a statement thus constituted a not-so-veiled attack on the Saudi regime, whose very existence was supposedly predicated on the suppression of shirk and the propagation of the Wahhabi message. The statement on Yemen preceded the distribution of several cassettes featuring al-Hawali and al-'Awda, in which they attacked the regime's position on the Yemeni civil war.[33]

The wave of arrests following al-Mas'ari's April 1994 flight to London escalated in August and, as occurred previously, was concentrated in Qasim province.[34] On September 9, the authorities detained al-Hawali, prompting al-'Awda—who feared he might also be detained—to go into hiding in Riyadh. He reappeared on September 11 leading a twenty-car motorcade to Burayda. Upon his arrival at the mosque where he preached, he roused his followers to oppose the regime's efforts to stifle the opposition. He was then called to the governor's mansion in Burayda but, again fearing arrest, arrived in a convoy that the CDLR reported comprised five hundred followers. Al-'Awda refused to sign a document agreeing to desist from opposition activity and instead left for his mosque, where large gatherings took place that day and the next. His supporters submitted a petition to the Council of Senior 'Ulama, accusing the council of complicity in the regime's violation of human rights and freedom of expression and assembly. The CDLR reported that the petition contained twenty thousand signatures, though that was probably an exaggeration.

On September 13, security forces arrested al-'Awda in Burayda. More mass protests followed at the governor's mansion in Burayda. "Traditional clerics" tried to persuade the people not to protest, but "new generation clerics" won the day, commented the CDLR, which estimated the number of protesters to be eight thousand.[35] Foreign diplomats in Riyadh reported that five hundred activists had occupied the governor's quarters.[36] Protests also continued for several days in Riyadh. Al-Hawali was rearrested on September 16, after appearing before gatherings of the Ghamid and Zahran tribes. The CDLR reported about thirteen hundred arrests during this time, yet the regime and the Saudi press initially made no reference to the events.[37]

Then the Kata'ib al-Iman, which was previously unknown, issued an ultimatum to the Saudi authorities. It threatened that, if al-'Awda was not released, it would destroy Western institutions; kidnap U.S. citizens, Saudi royal family members, and security personnel; and attack corporations owned by the Saudi royal family. "All the Arabian Peninsula is an open theater for our Jihad operations," declared the organization. "It is never acceptable that Christians and Jews are wandering freely in the Peninsula while the 'ulama are held in prison."[38]

In its own response to the arrests, the CDLR viciously lashed out:

> It is ironic that a government which harbors and protects killers, rapists, blackmailers, and gangsters, and which has squandered a $120 bn. surplus and is now saddled with a $90 bn. deficit on useless armaments and weapons, and on personal pleasures of individual members of the Saudi royal family to satisfy their insatiable carnal desires, should point an accusing finger at two decent, religious, noble citizens of the holy land, men who are totally innocent of such crimes.[39]

As a result of the demonstrations, the U.S. and British embassies issued warnings to their nationals to take "sensible precautions."[40]

Following the September arrests, a document entitled "The Scholars' Requests" shed light on some of al-'Awda's and al-Hawali's ideas. As in similar documents published by the radical fundamentalists in Saudi Arabia since the Iraqi invasion of Kuwait, the scholars called for the "complete implementation of the shari'a and the cancellation of all laws and regulations which disagree with it, "justice and equality" without regard to social position, and the support of religious institutions. Their call for Saudi Arabia and its 'ulama to be the bearers of the message of tawhid to the world, carrying the Wahhabi da'wa beyond the borders of the kingdom, was particularly important: "Define a true and specific message for the country which is summarized in supporting Islam and Muslims and raising the flag of Islam so that this message appears in internal and foreign policies of the country." Moreover, the statement called for

> devising foreign policy on the basis of carrying the Islamic message to the world and to protect the interests of the

Ummah away from organizations and international institutions that are against Shari'a; to take on the plight of
Muslims everywhere and to guide the embassies to enable
them to carry out these duties."[41]

Such a view was reminiscent of Ibn Sa'ud's *Ikhwan*, followers of
the Wahhabi creed in the early twentieth century who sought
to expand its influence in the Arabian Peninsula and beyond.
Indeed, there are several parallels between the new radical
fundamentalists and the Ikhwan. Both represented an ultra-
conservative constituency seeking to maintain the continuity
of Wahhabism as a living, guiding force in all aspects of policy,
foreign and domestic. Even the Ikhwan tradition of carrying
arms was echoed in the scholars' demands, in the guise of re-
jecting Saudi dependence on the United States. The radical
fundamentalists demanded that the government

> build a strong army with numerous resources of arms and
> weapons and to train young men in large numbers; to train
> whoever is able to carry weapons from the Ummah [com-
> munity of believers] so that the whole Ummah can become
> an army in reserve if the need arises; to work hard at manu-
> facturing our own weapons.[42]

Al-Hawali held democracy and elections in contempt, referring to Jean-Jacques Rousseau as an "enemy of religion" and
stating, "For you to be elected you need money, lots of it. And
once elected you are beholden to the interests of the rich
and neglect the downtrodden."[43] In Saudi Arabia, the arguments between the radical fundamentalists and the regime
were more frequently about corruption, accountability, and
power sharing than about the implementation of democracy.
Indeed, Interior Minister Prince Nayif used language similar
to al-Hawali when questioned about democracy: "We are convinced that not a single deputy is elected to parliament
because of his abilities but rather because of his money, or
his membership in a political party."[44]

Al-'Awda was particularly eloquent in defense of the rights
of the 'ulama to engage freely and independently in *da'wa*

(preaching). In a recording of a lecture entitled *sina'at al-mawt* (The Manufacture of Death), which he presented shortly before his arrest,[45] al-'Awda stated that the government had introduced un-Islamic measures to prevent preachers from engaging in da'wa and that reform would not occur until Muslims were ready to endure hardships for their beliefs. He demanded the right to preach freely and asserted his willingness to pay the price, lest the preachers be accused of acting only for their own egos.

> Where are the thousands of doctors, professors, and university students on whom millions were spent to further their education? The educated people are being told to stop thinking! This is unacceptable. It is every human's right to exercise his intellect to improve the community surrounding him.

Al-'Awda railed against the attempts of the regime to marginalize the ideas of the younger 'ulama. "Our religion," declared al-'Awda, "was not meant to be only confined to corners of a particular mosque. It came to teach us how to structure our economy and how to invest our money."[46]

Meanwhile, the CDLR tried to fill the void following the arrest of the Awakening Shaykhs. It exposed the perceived Islamic illegitimacy of the regime ('adam shar'iyyat al-nizam), while regaling its readers with spicy stories of the corruption and peccadilloes of the royal family. In a closely reasoned eight-part series, the CDLR tried to prove that the Al Sa'ud had introduced political and religious innovations that were not in line with God's law, such as various committees and royal decrees that had no basis in the shari'a. Anyone who complied with these laws, or forced others to do so, was himself a *kafir kharij min al-milla* (an unbeliever who had withdrawn from the community).[47] The regime was compared to a "putrefying corpse" that could not acknowledge that the nation was educated and knowledgeable about its political and constitutional rights.[48] The "Prince of the Month" series featured Defense Minister Sultan bin 'Abd Al-'Aziz as "the world's biggest and best known skimmer."[49] The CDLR claimed that

Prince Nayif had appointed his eight-year-old son as a deputy to the head of a delegation to Bahrain and Tunisia. "Why do [the Al Sa'ud] persist in their indifference and contempt for the people even after the Nation has made no secret of its hatred of their illegitimate rule?" queried the CDLR.[50]

In 1995 the CDLR became more strident in its attacks on the *'ulama al-sulta* (regime's scholars) who legitimized the royal family's activities; it juxtaposed the regime's scholars with the CDLR's own 'ulama, the anonymous *al-qiyadat al-shar'iyya* (Islamically legitimate leadership). The CDLR warned Bin Baz that if he did not offer clarifications to their satisfaction, "he will remain a tool in the hands of the Al Sa'ud and party to their oppression and tyranny."[51] Citing Ibn Taymiyya, a four-teenth-century Damascene cleric whose fundamentalist views have inspired modern fundamentalists, the CDLR said the official 'ulama who supported those acting contrary to shari'a were no better than the violators themselves.[52] If they contin-ued, despite the "evidence" of anti-Islamic legal practices the CDLR cited, the official 'ulama would be guilty of a serious sin, because of their knowledge of shari'a.[53] If that were deemed to be the case, the CDLR continued, then the establishment 'ulama's fatwas should be ignored.[54] The "scholars of Al Sa'ud," intoned the CDLR, had been "completely disregarded and scorned by the legitimate leaders, who fear none but Allah with regard to speaking the truth."[55]

The CDLR also attacked the regime's new economic poli-cies, which cut subsidies for utilities and wheat farmers—policies that international financial experts had recommended. The subsidies reduction was meant, said the CDLR, "to make up for the cost of Al Sa'ud's colossal em-bezzlement from the state's resources."[56]

After the November 1995 bombing of the Riyadh head-quarters of the U.S. mission to the Saudi Arabian National Guard, known as the Office of the Program Manager (OPM/ SANG, see chapter 5) the CDLR chose its words more care-fully. CDLR London representative Sa'd al-Faqih stated that the bombing was a "natural result" of Saudi oppression that had left young Saudis with "no means to express themselves other than violence."[57] The British Foreign Office quoted CDLR activist Muhammad al-Mas'ari saying that the installation bombed was a "legitimate target" because the United States operated it. Al-Mas'ari denied this allegation, stating that he had said it was "the perception of the common man that [U.S. troops] are a legitimate target."[58]

Although the CDLR clearly did not support the royal family, there was a distinct attempt to place Crown Prince 'Abdallah in a better light than the others. 'Abdallah, the CDLR reported, had not become involved in the infighting of the Sudayris, the full brothers of King Fahd. After Fahd became ill in November 1995, the CDLR reported that Prince Sultan, the defense minister, had convened the 'ulama to prevent 'Abdallah from assuming the throne. In a "Sudayri conspiracy," the CDLR maintained that Fahd had insisted that SANG, which 'Abdallah commanded, conduct maneuvers in Qasim as a show of force and to make the people of Qasim hate 'Abdallah, because "there was no evidence of his involvement in the Government's crimes against the people of Qasim."[59] Such talk may have indicated a greater CDLR affinity for 'Abdallah, who projected an image of a simple, pious man of the people, or perhaps a desire on the part of the CDLR to curry favor with the non-Sudayri crown prince, who might soon be king.

Al-Mas'ari offered few of the specifics of the regime he wished to establish. In CDLR circulars, the theme was merely that a more "Islamic" system needed to be founded. While speaking in Westminster to a British audience, however, al-Mas'ari talked about his preference for "Islamic democracy," with free municipal and national elections and universal suffrage. He spoke of an independent judiciary and stressed that women should have their Islamic legal rights, including the right to drive.[60] Although al-Mas'ari might have been a bit more worldly than the Awakening Shaykhs, as he came from an educated middle class that had ideas about a government more responsive to popular sentiment and more economically responsible, his ideas had more in common with those of the Awakening Shaykhs than differences. Both groups opposed the Al Sa'ud and the establishment 'ulama and desired the "proper" application of the shari'a. What al-Mas'ari had done was simply "repackage" the message for much of the more modern but still strongly fundamentalist middle class, as well as for the West. For instance, like Sudan's Hasan al-Turabi, al-Mas'ari supported "women's rights," but one is left wondering if, in practice, al-Mas'ari's desired regime would result in setbacks for women, as in al-Turabi's Sudan.[61]

The Split in the CDLR and the Birth of New Groups

Although Muhammad al-Mas'ari successfully halted British efforts to deport him, his organization experienced an acrimonious rupture. On March 5, 1996, both al-Mas'ari and the CDLR's London representative, Sa'd al-Faqih, issued communiqués expelling the other from the group. Al-Mas'ari accused al-Faqih of refusing to fund the former's legal struggle against deportation and of changing the locks on the CDLR's headquarters. Moreover, he said al-Faqih was in contact with Crown Prince 'Abdallah and Saudi intelligence, had compromised activists inside the country, and had attempted to blackmail al-Mas'ari. Accordingly, said the statement, the "CDLR Shura Assembly" in Burayda and the founding chairman of the CDLR (al-Mas'ari's father, 'Abdallah) had canceled al-Faqih's membership in the organization. Muhammad al-Mas'ari was now both spokesman and secretary-general of the group. Al-Faqih issued a more laconic statement, which dismissed Muhammad al-Mas'ari and appointed himself as official spokesman in al-Mas'ari's place; he also denied the existence of the Shura Assembly. Both factions issued their own versions of *al-Huquq* issue 90, with different dates.[62] Despite mediation efforts by other radical Sunni groups in Britain, the two factions officially split on March 11 into the CDLR, led by al-Mas'ari, and the Movement for Islamic Reform in Arabia (MIRA), led by al-Faqih.[63]

Their dispute centered on al-Mas'ari's participation in two groups considered by many Islamists-from different countries to be bizarre, unreliable, and fanatical: *Hizb al-Tahrir* (the Liberation Party) and a breakaway faction, *al-Muhajirun* (the Emigrés). These organizations did not recognize the Islamic legitimacy of any regime, including those in Sudan and Iran, and proposed an unnamed member of their organization to rule the entire Muslim *umma* (nation). Hizb al-Tahrir operated freely in London, although it had at one time been associated with terrorist activity in Jordan. According to an exchange on a "Muslims only" e-mail list, al-Jazirah-Net, the controversy surrounding al-Mas'ari's contact with these groups began to surface in 1995 when al-Mas'ari admitted and defended his membership in Hizb al-Tahrir but noted that the membership had since been suspended (Hizb al-Tahrir, apparently, did not allow simultaneous membership in other bodies). According to al-Mas'ari, Hizb al-Tahrir was beyond reproach in its approach to Islam and in its support of the Islamic movement in Saudi Arabia.[64]

Confirmation of al-Mas'ari's empathy toward Hizb al-Tahrir came from 'Umar Bakri Muhammad, a Syrian former leader of Hizb al-Tahrir who left to found al-Muhajirun. He said al-Mas'ari had been a member of Hizb al-Tahrir while still in Saudi Arabia and, once in Britain, joined al-Muhajirun and served on its supreme shura council. As for al-Faqih, said Muhammad, he had been a member of the Muslim Brotherhood.[65]

The CDLR seemed to deteriorate during 1996. The split resulted in al-Mas'ari losing most of his funding, and he was reduced to appeals over the Internet. Either because of his alliance with al-Muhajirun and other London-based extremists or for financial reasons, he allowed other groups to distribute their messages on the CDLR's e-mail list; these groups included the Bangladeshi Muslim Literary Circle, which used the list to attack Israel, the United States, and the rulers of Bangladesh. Al-Mas'ari joined al-Muhajirun and the Bangladeshi Muslim Literary Circle in signing statements calling on the Organization of the Islamic Conference (OIC) to recognize the independence of the Turkish enclave on Cyprus and attacking France for its effort to ban women from wearing the *hijab* (head scarf), an action the groups termed a declaration of war on Islam. The Palestinian Hamas organization, the Muslim Brotherhood, the Algerian group FIS, and the Tunisian al-Nahda organization all rejected al-Muhajirun, and, by implication, al-Mas'ari.[66]

Al-Mas'ari declared bankruptcy in January 1997 because many of his former backers had shifted support to al-Faqih. The CDLR leader tried to raise money through his alliance with extremist Islamist organizations in London, including al-Muhajirun. Together they formed an organization called Muslims Against Tyranny (MAST, "as in Fahd MAST go," they declared) to raise money for the CDLR. Al-Mas'ari flooded the Internet with appeals for funds.[67]

In the meantime, MIRA developed into an organization that presented a more reasonable image than al-Mas'ari's CDLR. Its statements dealt only with Saudi Arabia and not the myriad Islamic issues to which the CDLR gave voice. Al-Faqih's organization claimed to be the true voice of the reform movement in Saudi Arabia and stood firmly behind the imprisoned radical 'ulama. Al-Faqih argued that Saudi youth sought advice from all of the 'ulama, establishment and radical, but the regime had made the mistake of imprisoning the radical leaders and using the establishment clerics to support state decisions contrary to Islam. This action discredited the establishment 'ulama, leaving the youth without leadership:

> As a result, provocation continued to build up against the young who had wanted guidance but were left to decide and make *fatawa* [religious legal rulings] for themselves. Another [problem] was created by the bad economic conditions resulting in the spread of unemployment, deprivation, and suffering, seen against the background of luxury and abundance enjoyed by the ruling family. That created the feeling in some of the young that they had nothing to fear and nothing to lose.[68]

Currently, MIRA remains the only organized voice of the radical fundamentalist opposition in Saudi Arabia. Unlike the CDLR, al-Faqih's organization maintains an up-to-date website, complete with software allowing the organization to transmit weekly broadcasts.

Another Saudi overseas opposition group, the Committee Against Corruption in Saudi Arabia (CACSA), emerged in 1996. Although the liberal–modernist sector of the Saudi opposition had raised its voice occasionally, CACSA's founding marked its most organized attempt to present a united front. The identity of the organization was obscure, but it maintained a sophisticated website—www.saudhouse.com—complete with biographical information about the Saudi royal family, many stories of corruption, and full-text copies of books critical of the regime. The organization attacked Wahhabi "fundamentalism" and seemed aimed at a U.S. audience rather than at a Saudi one.

The overseas Saudi opposition lost much of its momentum after the split in the CDLR. Financial difficulties were at the core of the problem, and al-Faqih likely wanted to assume a lower profile after the problems encountered by al-Mas'ari.

Notes

1. In Arabic, *Lajnat al-Difa' 'an al-Huquq al-Shar'iyya.* A more meaningful translation would have been "Committee for the Defense of Islamically-sanctioned (*shar'i*) Rights," as the use of the term *shar'iyya,* while carrying with it the meaning of legitimate, meant also rights associated with or guaranteed by Islamic law; the founders of the committee most certainly wanted to convey the double entendre. Committee for the Defense of Legitimate Rights (CDLR) is used here as the name by which the founders wanted the committee to be known in English.

2. See *al-Wa'y,* January 1993; Saudi Press Agency (SPA), May 13, 1993, in "Human Rights Committee Leaders Relieved of Jobs," Foreign Broadcast Information Service Near East and South Asia daily report FBIS-NES-93-092, May 14, 1993, p. 19; *al-Ribat,* May 19–25, 1993; Middle East Studies Association of North America, *MESA Newsletter* (August 1993).

3. Agence France-Presse, May 13, in "Rights Committee Leader Briefs Diplomats," FBIS-NES-93-092, May 14, 1993, p. 19.

4. According to the Movement for Islamic Reform in Arabia (MIRA), a group which broke with the CDLR, the CDLR appointed Muhammad al-Mas'ari only as the spokesman for the group. See MIRA, *History of*

Dissent: The Story of Islamic Dissent in Arabia, chapter 11, "The Committee for the Defence of Legitimate Rights," online at http://www.miraserve.com/chap11.html.

5. BBC World Service, May 6, 1993, in "Human Rights Activist Discusses Group's Aims," FBIS-NES-93-096, May 20, 1993, p. 13.

6. On this repackaging, see "Islam Is the Power of the Future," in Martin Kramer, *Arab Awakening and Islamic Revival: The Politics of Ideas in the Middle East* (New Brunswick, N.J.: Transaction Publishers, 1996), pp. 141–159.

7. Agence France-Presse, May 7, 1993, in "Human Rights Group to Fight 'Oppression, Injustice'" FBIS-NES-93-089, May 11, 1993, p. 24.

8. Agence France-Presse, May 9, 1993, in "Leaders Informed of King's Dissatisfaction," FBIS-NES-93-089, May 11, 1993, p. 25; *Gulf States Newsletter,* May 17, 1993; MIRA, *History of Dissent,* chapter 11.

9. See both *'Ukaz* and *al-Hayat,* May 13, 1993; SPA, May 12, 1993, in "Senior Ulema Council Calls Rights Committee Illegal," FBIS-NES-93-091, May 13, 1993, p. 21.

10. See SPA, May 13, 1993, in "Rights Committee Leader Briefs Diplomats," FBIS-NES-93-092, May 14, 1993, p. 19; *Le Monde,* May 15, 1993. The arrests were never confirmed by Saudi authorities. For additional information, see Agence France-Presse, May 15–18, June 17, and August 9, 1993; *al-Quds al-'Arabi,* September 4-5, 1993; *Arabia Monitor,* August 1993; U.S. State Department, *Country Report on Human Rights Practices for 1993* (Washington: U.S. Department of State, February 1994). The State Department reported that Saudi Arabia released Muhammad al-Mas'ari in November 1993.

11. See *al-Quds al-'Arabi,* June 4, 1993 (quoted here); and *al-Muharrir,* July 19, 1993. See also *al-Safir,* June 5, 1993.

12. *CDLR Communiqué,* no. 5, April 23, 1994. See also *CDLR Communiqué,* no. 6, April 25, 1994; *CDLR Communiqué,* no. 7, May 1, 1994; and *CDLR Communiqué,* no. 8, May 8, 1994. CDLR documents are in author's possession or can be obtained by email request from cdlr@cdlr.net.

13. *Guardian* (London), November 28, 1994; *Daily Telegraph,* November 29, 1994; *The Independent,* December 12, 1994; *CDLR Monitor,* no. 24, December 2, 1994; *CDLR Monitor,* no. 26, December 16, 1994.

14. Reuters, January 4, 1996; *Financial Times,* January 5, 1996.

15. Associated Press, March 6, 1996.

16. *Wall Street Journal,* April 19, 1996.

17. It should be stressed that there is no way to verify these or other allegations against the Al Sa'ud. Many such allegations are usually common knowledge among Saudis and Westerners who deal with Saudi Arabia. They are brought here as examples of the nature of the CDLR's charges and not as endorsement of their veracity.

18. See *CDLR Monitor,* no. 1, May 30, 1994; *al-Huquq,* no. 1, May 29, 1994.

19. See *CDLR Monitor,* no. 7, July 11, 1994; *CDLR Monitor,* no. 9, July 25, 1994.

20. See *al-Huquq,* no. 3, June 11, 1994; *CDLR Monitor,* no. 3, June 13, 1994; *CDLR Monitor,* no. 6, July 4, 1994.

21. "The CDLR abides by the method of peaceful and constructive criticism and dissociates [sic] itself from all and any attempts to effect reform by force"; CDLR, "Introduction," May 18, 1994.

22. *CDLR Communiqué,* no. 3, April 20, 1994; *CDLR Monitor,* no. 4, June 20, 1994; CDLR press release, September 14, 1994.

23. CDLR Introduction, May 18, 1994.

24. *CDLR Monitor,* no. 20, November 4, 1994.

25. *Guardian* (London), November 4, 1994. Al-Mas'ari later said, "If by fundamentalism you mean sticking to the principles of the Koran, yes, I am a fundamentalist. If you mean the frozen positions invented by the government clerics, then definitely I am not," *New Yorker,* November 28, 1994.

26 *CDLR Monitor,* no. 20, November 4, 1994.

27. Ibid. On this council, see chapter 7.

28. *CDLR Monitor,* no. 17, October 14, 1994.

29. Muhammad Al-Rifa'i, *Al-Mashru' al-Islahi fi al-Sa'udiyya,* pp. 39–45; *al-Hayat, al-Sharq al-Awsat,* September 27, 1994; *al-Majalla,* October 9–15, 1994.

30. *Daily Telegraph,* June 27, 1994; *Washington Post,* June 30, 1994.

31. Shaykh Salman bin Fahd al-'Awda, letter, MSANEWS, July 3, 1994.

32. CDLR press release, July 5, 1994; see also Al-Rifa'i, *Al-Mashru' al-Islahi fi al-Sa'udiyya,* pp. 154–156.

33. Al-Rifa'i, *Al-Mashru' al-Islahi fi al-Sa'udiyya,* p. 69.

34. *CDLR Communiqué*, no. 13, August 13, 1994; *CDLR Communiqué*, no. 14, August 21, 1994; *CDLR Communiqué*, no. 15, August 28, 1994; *CDLR Monitor*, no. 15, September 9, 1994.

35. *CDLR Communiqué*, no. 17, September 11, 1994; CDLR press release, September 14, 1994.

36. Youssef M. Ibrahim, "Saudi Arabia Cracks Down on Islamic Militants, Seizing Many," *New York Times*, September 22, 1994, p. A5. The Burayda incident is also covered extensively in Al-Rifa'i, *Al-Mashru' al-Islahi fi al-Sa'udiyya*, pp. 70–71.

37. CDLR press release, September 19, 1994; Al-Rifa'i, *Al-Mashru' al-Islahi fi al-Sa'udiyya*, p. 71.

38 CDLR press release, September 14, 1994. The CDLR was the only source of this announcement.

39. CDLR press release, September 28, 1994, responding to an official Saudi communiqué.

40. CDLR press release, September 14, 1994; Associated Press, September 18, 1994.

41. CDLR press release, September 24, 1994.

42. CDLR press release, September 25, 1994.

43. Emmanuel Sivan, "Eavesdropping on Islam," *Middle East Quarterly* 2 (March 1995), pp. 13–24 (quoting excerpts from two speeches recorded on cassettes by al-Hawali).

44. Deutsche Press Agentur (DPA), December 10, 1994 (citing Nayif interview with *Der Spiegel*).

45. The choice of this title signified his devotion to his cause and was reminiscent of an essay with the same title by Sami Shawkat, the Iraqi nationalist and director general of Iraq's Ministry of Education in the 1930s. The essay was the text of a speech he gave to a group of students preparing to undergo basic military training. Sami Shawkat, "The Profession of Death," in Sylvia Haim, ed., *Arab Nationalism: An Anthology* (Berkeley: University of California Press, 1976), pp. 97–99.

46. The translated transcript of the taped lecture "From Behind Bars" is available from the Movement for Islamic Reform in Arabia (MIRA), located online at www.miraserve.com/ffbars.zip; and as *sina'at al-mawt* (Death Workmanship) from Azzam Publications, a jihadist organization, located online at www.azzam.com.

47. See *al-Huquq*, no. 49, May 24, 1995; *CDLR Monitor*, no. 49, May 26, 1995.

48. *CDLR Monitor*, no. 31, January 20, 1995.

49. CDLR, "Prince of the Month—Sultan bin Abdel Aziz," 1995.

50. *CDLR Monitor*, no. 30, January 13, 1995.

51. *CDLR Monitor*, no. 31, January 20, 1995.

52. *CDLR Monitor*, no. 54, June 30, 1995.

53. *CDLR Monitor*, no. 55, July 7, 1995; *al-Huquq*, no. 55, July 5, 1995.

54. See *al-Huquq*, no. 58, July 26, 1995; *CDLR Monitor*, no. 58, July 28, 1995.

55. *CDLR Monitor*, no. 42, April 7, 1995.

56. *CDLR Monitor*, no. 29, January 6, 1995; *CDLR Monitor*, no. 34, February 10, 1995.

57. Agence France-Presse, November 14, 1995, in "Rights Group Expects More Bombings," FBIS-NES-95-219, November 14, 1995, p. 24.

58. Reuters, November 16, 1995.

59. *CDLR Monitor*, no. 40, March 24, 1995; *CDLR Monitor*, no. 76, November 29, 1995; *CDLR Monitor*, no. 78, December 15, 1995; *CDLR Communiqué*, no. 42, December 11, 1995.

60. See *al-Quds al-'Arabi*, January 19, 1995.

61. See Amir Weissbrod, *Turabi: Spokesman of Radical Islam* (in Hebrew), Dayan Center Papers no. 124 (Tel Aviv: Moshe Dayan Center, 1999).

62. CDLR press release by Al-Mas'ari, March 4, 1996 (English press release, March 5, 1996); *CDLR Communiqué*, no. 44 (by Faqih), March 7, 1996; *al-Huquq* (by Faqih), no. 90, March 7, 1996. See also the fax statement issued by 'Abdallah bin Sulayman Al-Mas'ari, "founder of the committee and chairman of the CDLR," in Riyadh, 17 Shawwal 1416 (March 7, 1996); and the "members of the *majlis al-shura* of the CDLR in the Arabian Peninsula," in Burayda, 17 Shawwal 1416 [March 7, 1996]; *al-Islah*, no. 1, March 16, 1996. All documents are in the author's possession.

63. Joint MIRA–CDLR statement, March 11, 1996.

64. "Dispute Around CDLR," an exchange on al-Jazirah-Net distributed by the CDLR over MSANEWS, October 6, 1996.

65. See *al-Sharq al-Awsat*, March 7, 1996.

66. See, for example, CDLR New Year's Address, September 26—MSANEWS, September 27, 1996; Compass News Service, August 23, 1996; *al-Sharq al-Awsat*, September 9, 1996; *Ruz al-Yusuf*, September 9, 1996.

67. See *al-Sharq al-Awsat*, January 9, 1997; *Financial Times*, January 12, 1997; *Middle East*, February 1997; and various CDLR communiqués sent via Internet to services including MSANEWS and Usenet groups, dated April 2, May 23, and December 27, 1997 (copies of which are in author's possession).

68. See *al-Islah*, no. 16, July 1, 1996.

Chapter 5

The Saudi 'Afghans' Strike

The methods that the "Awakening Shaykhs" and groups such as the Committee for the Defense of Legitimate Rights (CDLR) and the Movement for Islamic Reform in Arabia (MIRA) utilized were essentially nonviolent and were designed to change the government through vocal opposition by refuting both Al Saʿud's monopoly on Islam and the ruling family's ensuing claim to legitimacy. The groups' techniques included distributing audiocassettes and submitting closely argued petitions of advice and exhortation. But the *mujahidin*, Saudi veterans of the war against the Soviet Union in Afghanistan, had a different idea of the course to follow.

The Rise of Violence

On November 13, 1995, a bomb ripped through central Riyadh. Initial Saudi reports noted only that the explosion had killed several Americans, without noting the nature of the target.[1] But U.S. officials said the Americans killed had been employed by the Office of the Program Manager of the Saudi Arabian National Guard (OPM/SANG), and other sources said that the building damaged was the three-story SANG communications center, which was manned by almost fifty U.S. advisers. For the past twenty-two years, the U.S. Army had run a program, funded by the U.S. Army Materiel Command, to provide U.S. civilian and military personnel to train the SANG.[2] The explosion killed five Americans and two Indians and injured almost sixty others. Among the Americans killed were one active serviceman with the U.S. Army and four civilian employees;[3] the five had been among the very visible contingent of U.S. troops in the Najdi heartland, which had included uniformed U.S. soldiers shopping in Riyadh

73

supermarkets, and a U.S. military radio station based in Dhahran that broadcast U.S. news and rock-and-roll across the breadth of the country all the way to Jeddah.[4]

The site had apparently been chosen some time prior to the blast. One local resident said pamphlets had been circulated in the neighborhood about three months earlier, warning that foreigners who supported the Saudi ruling family were in danger.[5] A British Embassy official confirmed that "a couple of months" previously the embassy had received a warning from a militant Islamic group; U.S. ambassador to Saudi Arabia Raymond Mabus confirmed that the United States had received similar threats.[6]

Three previously unknown groups claimed responsibility for the bombing. The first was the *Numur al-Khalij* (Tigers of the Gulf), which placed two telephone calls to Agence France-Presse in Nicosia, Cyprus. "The attacks will continue until the departure of the last American soldier," said the caller.[7]

The second group to claim credit for the attack was the *Harakat al-Taghyir al-Islamiyya, al-Janah al-Jihadi fi al-Jazira al-'Arabiyya* (Islamic Change Movement, the Jihad Wing in the Arabian Peninsula). This organization had sent faxes to news agencies and the London-based *al-Quds al-'Arabi* in April and July 1995 threatening to carry out operations against the "Crusader forces" unless they left the Arabian Peninsula; if not, the foreigners, as well as Saudi forces and members of the royal family, would become "legitimate targets." The communiqué accused the Saudi regime of fighting Islam and legitimate reformers and preachers. The April statement established June 28 as the deadline for foreign forces to leave Saudi Arabia.[8]

The third group to claim responsibility was the *Munazzamat Ansar Allah al-Muqatila* (Militant Partisans of God Organization), which claimed that the explosion was "the first of our jihad operations." It demanded that the United States leave the Arabian Peninsula and release Sunni fundamentalist activists 'Umar 'Abd al-Rahman and Ramzi Yusuf (charged in the World Trade Center bombing), as well as Palestinian Hamas official Musa Abu Marzuq. It further condemned the

Saudi regime for imposing restrictions on Muslim *'ulama* (clerics) and not applying the *shari'a* (Islamic law). The organization's communiqué declared that the group would declare *bay'a 'ala al-mawt fi sabil allah* (an allegiance to death in the path of God) should its demands be refused.[9]

The attack was then the largest of its kind in Saudi history. Saudi officials were quick to point out that the blast was not indicative of difficulties in the kingdom and did "not reflect in any way on the stability of the kingdom of Saudi Arabia."[10] Yet, the regime could not hide this type of opposition activity from its citizens. The Saudi press was thus obligated to cover the incident fully, and the regime admitted that it suspected Saudi citizens of being responsible.[11] The bombing was a significant escalation in radical Sunni activity, which had been nonviolent for many years. In April 1995, a bomb had exploded in front of the residence of the Saudi Ambassador to Greece, killing one person, but the incident went largely unreported.[12] There was also a report that the Saudis had foiled an attempt to bomb the Defense Ministry and Petromin Oil building in Riyadh in November 1995, a report the Saudi government denied vehemently.[13]

The first break in the investigation occurred in early February 1996, when Pakistan announced it had deported Hasan al-Surayhi, a Saudi citizen who had been a *mujahid* (holy warrior) in Afghanistan, to Saudi Arabia.[14] The Arab "Afghans,"[15] as the mujahidin who had fought the Soviets in Afghanistan are called, were behind many of the Islamic terrorist attacks worldwide in the 1990s and received funding from Saudi radical fundamentalist Usama bin Ladin. Since returning from Afghanistan, they have been involved in Islamic struggles from Bosnia to Central Asia to Egypt. Some believe there may be almost 5,000 Saudi "Afghans." During the war in Afghanistan, the Saudi leadership had encouraged them and had funded the mujahidin. Leading cleric Shaykh 'Abd Al-'Aziz bin Baz and Shaykh Muhammad al-Salih al-'Uthaymin also reportedly encouraged the fighters.[16]

Al-Surayhi was never seen again, but he may have provided essential information to the Saudis. On April 22,

Minister of Interior Prince Nayif bin 'Abd al-'Aziz announced
the arrest of four suspects who had been charged with the
bombing.[17] The nearly identical confessions of the four—
Riyad Sulayman Ishaq al-Hajiri, 'Abd al-'Aziz Fahd Nasir
al-Mu'aththam, Muslih 'Ali 'A'idh al-Shamrani, and Khalid
Ahmad Ibrahim al-Sa'id—were read personally from prepared
statements on Saudi TV, as Muslih al-Shamrani pointed to
diagrams and maps of the operation. Al-Mu'aththam reported
that he had decided that the U.S. presence in Saudi Arabia
warranted an act of *jihad,* or holy war. He and the others obtained explosives from Yemen, donned "Pakistani" clothes,
and drove the car to the OPM/SANG building. They then set
the timer and fled in another vehicle.[18]

All four young men were in their twenties. Al-Mu'aththam
said when he was younger he adopted religious ideas and
grew his beard and began wearing the shorter *thawb* (a long
gown worn by men in the Gulf countries) characteristic of
the *Ikhwan,* Ibn Sa'ud's devoted shock troops during the early
part of the twentieth century. Three of them said they had
been trained in Afghanistan and had fought the Soviets there.
They also stated that they had been influenced by 'Issam Tahir
al-Maqdisi, known as "Abu Muhammad," the leader of the
extremist Jordanian organization *Bay'at al-Imam* (Fealty to the
Religious Leader), who was imprisoned near Amman, as well
as by Bin Ladin and by the CDLR's Muhammad al-Mas'ari.
Al-Mu'aththam declared that he had visited al-Maqdisi several times in the Hashemite Kingdom and that he was
impressed by the ideas of these people who pronounced the
kufr (infidelity) of the Arab and Islamic countries and of Saudi
Arabia's Council of Senior 'Ulama.[19] In his televised confession, al-Mu'aththam condemned the Saudi kingdom for not
adhering to the shari'a and for being an ally of non-Muslim
countries. He also attacked the Council of Senior 'Ulama for
acquiescing in these policies.[20]

In his statement, al-Shamrani said he had grown his beard
and cut his *thawb* for similar reasons. He became acquainted
with a circle of friends who were followers of 'Abdallah bin
al-Jibrin, a high-ranking *'alim* (cleric) who had been one of

the CDLR's founders. Al-Shamrani had joined the Saudi Army at the age of 16 but left after one year to fight in Afghanistan. According to his family, his tours of duty in Afghanistan turned him into a dedicated mujahid who often expressed his wish to have died there as a martyr. Al-Shamrani returned to the kingdom alienated by the regime he once served. The army would not take him back; he held menial jobs and sold produce from a street cart. One of al-Shamrani's brothers noted that "Muslih was convinced that he had to kill Americans."[21]

On May 31, 1996, al-Mu'aththam, al-Shamrani, and their friends were beheaded in central Riyadh. The Saudi Interior Ministry said, "We ask God to safeguard our country . . . and guide the Muslim youth and all the nation to see what their enemies plot against them."[22]

The Jihadist Trend: Usama bin Ladin and the Advice and Reform Committee

The men executed for the Riyadh bombing had been influenced by Usama bin Ladin, a son of the wealthy Saudi construction company magnate. Whereas the Awakening Shaykhs did not openly advocate violence, Bin Ladin did. He established the Consultative Organization to Defend Islamic Legal Rights in Khartoum, Sudan, where he was first based, and announced his support for the Committee for the Defense of Legitimate Rights (CDLR) in April 1994.[23] In London, Bin Ladin set up another organization, the *Hay'at al-Nasiha wal-Islah* (Advice and Reform Committee). He also began to publish three journals: *al-Yaman al-Kubra, al-Hijaz al-Kubra,* and *al-Shu'la.* These journals, all very similar, expressed support for the CDLR, attacked the Saudi regime, and were liberally sprinkled with Bin Ladin's picture. The avowed goal of the journals, as exemplified in a map published in each of them, was to abolish the Saudi state and divide the Arabian Peninsula into two states, "Greater Hijaz" and "Greater Yemen."[24]

In April 1994 the Saudis announced that they were stripping Bin Ladin of his citizenship. According to a statement by the Interior Ministry, Bin Ladin's "irresponsible behavior" contradicted "the kingdom's interests" and risked "harming its relations with fraternal countries."[25] Bin Ladin left Khartoum in May or June 1996 after Sudanese officials expelled him, following a deal they made with the Saudi government.[26] Under the auspices of the dominant Taliban militia, he established his headquarters in Afghanistan, from which he issued statements and met with journalists.

Bin Ladin represented the "jihadist" wing of the Saudi opposition. He was most explicit in calling for the expulsion of U.S. troops from the Arabian Peninsula, the "Land of Mecca and Medina." In a document entitled "A Declaration of War," Bin Ladin called the U.S. "occupation" of the Arabian Peninsula "the latest and greatest of . . . aggressions incurred by the Muslims . . . since the death of the Prophet." After *iman* (belief), there was no other duty for a Muslim more important than pushing out the Americans, he wrote. The Riyadh and Dhahran explosions (for more on the June 1996 Dhahran explosion, which killed nineteen U.S. servicemen, see chapter 6), he said, were a warning and a response to the collusion between the "Zionist–Crusader alliance" and the regime of King Fahd in imprisoning righteous 'ulama such as Safar bin 'Abd al-Rahman al-Hawali and Salman bin Fahd al-'Awda. Bin Ladin chided the armed forces and the SANG, saying the regime had usurped their role when it invited the Americans to defend the kingdom. "Not surprisingly," accused Bin Ladin, "the king himself wore a cross." The men of the armed forces should act in small, secret groups and conduct a guerrilla war against the U.S. troops, he advised. They should also facilitate the operations of the mujahidin by supplying them with arms, ammunition, and information. Although the regime bore responsibility for the dismal situation in the country, Bin Ladin declared, the people should concentrate their efforts on the "American enemy."[27]

Bin Ladin also taunted the United States, saying that it showed no courage when it did not respond to the killing of U.S. Marines in Beirut in 1983; when it withdrew its troops after a bombing attempt against Somalia-bound U.S. servicemen in Aden, Yemen, in December 1992; and when it left

Mogadishu in April 1993 after Somalis fired on its troops.[28] The United States linked Bin Ladin to the Aden attack in a special fact sheet.[29] Bin Ladin claimed credit for the attacks in Mogadishu as well, saying, "These were successful battles in which we inflicted big losses on the Americans. We used to hunt them down in Mogadishu."[30]

Bin Ladin stopped short of calling for violent attacks on the Saudi regime but harshly criticized it for imprisoning "our 'ulama"—a reference to al-'Awda and al-Hawali—leading to the loss of the regime's legitimacy.[31] The radical 'ulama were leaders to Bin Ladin and others like him. But the regime elevated men like Bin Baz to the rank of general mufti, Bin Ladin complained, because "of what it knows of his weakness and flexibility and the ease of influencing him. . . . So, a generation of youth [was] raised believing that the most pious and knowledgeable of people is Bin Baz." Bin Ladin continued,

> After this, the government began to strike, with the cane of Bin Baz, every corrective program which the scholars put forward . . . [and] it extracted a fatwa . . . to permit entry into the country . . . [by] the modern-day crusaders. Then it relied on a letter from him [Bin Baz] . . . to place the honest scholars in jail. The confidence of the people and the youth in Bin Baz was therefore shaken . . . while the confidence of the people in the working scholars, particularly those in the prisons, has been increased.[32]

In February 1997, Bin Ladin gave an interview to a British television program in which he threatened U.S. troops.[33] The Taliban, his protectors in his Afghanistan hideout, were reported to be wary of the publicity that Bin Ladin enjoyed, particularly after he gave an interview to CNN's Peter Arnett, which was broadcast in May. As part of an agreement later that month involving Saudi recognition of the Taliban government, the Taliban agreed to prevent Bin Ladin from making anti-Saudi statements.[34]

In mid-February 1998, the London newspaper *al-Quds al-'Arabi* published Bin Ladin's "Declaration of the World Islamic Front for Jihad against the Jews and the Crusaders."

After decrying the U.S. "occupation" of the Arabian Peninsula and the "Crusader–Jewish alliance" inflicting destruction
on Iraq, Bin Ladin issued a fatwa stating that "to kill Americans and their allies, both civil and military, is an individual
duty of every Muslim."[35] In August 1998, Bin Ladin's organization allegedly bombed the U.S. embassies in Kenya and
Tanzania. The United States then retaliated against alleged
Bin Ladin facilities in Sudan and Afghanistan.

Apprehending Bin Ladin is a priority for both the United
States and Saudi Arabia. Although most Saudi radical fundamentalists are not violent, it is difficult to assess the influence
of Bin Ladin in the kingdom or the extent of his involvement
in violent activities in Saudi Arabia. If the regime does not
find appropriate avenues for the Saudi "Afghans," there is a
danger that Bin Ladin may find more sympathizers.

Notes

1. Radio Riyadh, November 13, 1995, in "Riyadh Explosion Kills U.S. Personnel, Others—Cause of Blast Unknown," in Foreign Broadcast Information Service Near East and South Asia daily report FBIS-NES-95-218, November 13, 1995.

2. Reuters, November 13, 1995; *Financial Times*, November 14, 1995.

3. Associated Press, November 15, 1995; Reuters, November 23, 1995.

4. *New York Times*, August 15, 1996.

5. *Financial Times*, November 14, 1995.

6. Reuters, November 21, 1995; Associated Press, November 15, 1995; Agence France-Presse, November 20, 1995, in "Radio Monte Carlo Reports Riyadh Explosion—UK Embassy Received Similar Threat," FBIS-NES-96-001, November 20, 1995.

7. Agence France-Presse, November 13, 1995, in "Radio Monte Carlo Reports Riyadh Explosion—'Tigers of Gulf' Threatens Further At-tacks," FBIS-NES-96-001, November 13, 1995.

8. See *al-Quds al-'Arabi*, April 11, 1995; *al-Quds al-'Arabi*, July 3, 1995; *CDLR Monitor*, no. 43, April 14, 1995. All CDLR documents are in author's possession or can be obtained via email request to cdlr@cdlr.net.

9. See *al-Quds al-'Arabi*, November 15, 1995.

10. Saudi Press Agency (SPA), November 13, 1995.

11. Radio Monte Carlo, November 15, 1995.

12. Compass News Service, April 20, 1995; *al-Sharq al-Awsat*, April 21, 1995.

13. See *al-'Arabi* (Cairo), November 27, 1995; *al-Hayat*, November 28, 1995.

14. Associated Press, February 3, 1996; Reuters, February 3, 1996; Reuters, February 4, 1996; *al-Hayat*, February 5, 1996; *al-Sharq al-Awsat*, February 5, 1996.

15. *Jane's Intelligence Review*, April 1, 1995; *al-Majalla*, May 5–11, 1996.

16. See *al-Sirat al-Mustaqim*, August 1994 (interview with the Saudi *mujahid* "Abu 'Abd Al-'Aziz" Bahaziq), translated by MSANEWS, December 2, 1995, located online at www.mynet.net. Stories of the "martyrdom" of Saudi Afghans in Bosnia and for reports of arrests of Saudi *mujahidin* and their imprisonment are located online at http://www.azzam.com, which also carries links to Smith and Wesson's web site and others for those desiring knowledge about combat.

17. SPA, April 22, 1996.

18. See *al-Hayat*, April 23, 1996; *al-Sharq al-Awsat*, April 23, 1996; *al-Jazira*, June 1, 1996.

19. See *al-Wasat*, July 29, 1996 (interview with al-Maqdisi, confirming meeting with Mu'aththam).

20. See *al-Hayat*, April 23, 1996; *al-Sharq al-Awsat*, April 23, 1996; *al-Jazira*, June 1, 1996.

21. See *al-Jazira*, June 1, 1996; *Boston Globe*, July 7, 1996; *San Francisco Chronicle*, July 10, 1996.

22. SPA, May 31, 1996; Reuters, May 31, 1996; *al-Hayat*, June 1, 1996.

23. Dekmejian, "The Rise of Political Islam in Saudi Arabia."

24. See also the *Guardian*(London), August 3, 1994.

25. Agence France-Presse, April 7, 1994.

26. See *al-Wasat*, July 15–21, 1996 (interview with Sudanese minister of state Mustafa 'Uthman Isma'il); *al-Sharq al-Awsat*, June 18, 1996.

27. Usama Bin Ladin, "Declaration of War," MSANEWS; English translation located online at http://msanews.mynet.net/Scholars/Laden.

28. Usama Bin Ladin, "Declaration of War," MSANEWS; English translation located online at http://msanews.mynet.net/Scholars/Laden.

29. U.S. Department of State, "Fact Sheet on Usama bin Muhammad bin Awad bin Ladin," August 14, 1996.

30. See *al-Quds al-'Arabi,* November 27, 1996. Although most evidence during the year pointed to a Shi'i connection to the Dhahran bombing, U.S. Central Intelligence Agency (CIA) officials indicated that Bin Ladin was linked to the bombing. According to the report, Bin Ladin received congratulations for the attack from al-Mas'ari as well as from an Egyptian and a Palestinian Islamic extremist. *Washington Times,* October 24, 1996.

31. *Independent,* July 10, 1996.

32. Interview with Bin Ladin in *Nida al-Islam,* October–November 1996, online at http://www.islam.org.au. Bin Baz was appointed general mufti in July 1993; see chapter 7.

33. Reuters, February 20, 1997.

34. *Washington Post,* April 11, 1997; Reuters, May 11, 1997; CNN, May 11, 1997; *al-Ahram,* August 13, 1997; *al-Sharq al-Awsat,* April 11, 1997; Radio Riyadh, May 26, 1997.

35. See *al-Quds al-'Arabi,* February 23, 1998. See also Bernard Lewis, "License to Kill: Usama bin Ladin's Declaration of Jihad," *Foreign Affairs* 77 (November–December 1998), pp. 14–19 (containing partial translation and commentary on statement).

Chapter 6

Un(re)solved Mysteries: The Shi'i Opposition and the Bombing of the U.S. Barracks in Dhahran

---

Saudi Arabia's minority Shi'i population has never been a threat to the regime, but there were violent indigenous disturbances in 1979 and 1980, known to Shi'i activists as the *intifada* (uprising) of the Eastern Province, as well as Iranian-sponsored terrorism in that economically and politically deprived region.[1] After the Persian Gulf War of 1991, while reining in its radical Sunni fundamentalists, the Saudi regime also continued to take action against the Shi'is, which pleased the radical Sunnis. For Wahhabis, Shi'ism is *shirk* (polytheism), a practice which, by associating men and objects with God, is contrary to the creed of *tawhid* (the unity of God). Several Shi'i religious practices are banned in Saudi Arabia. Even questioning the government's treatment of Shi'ism has been cause for trouble. In March 1992, 'Abd al-Khaliq al-Janini and Mulla Turki Ahmad al-Turki were reportedly arrested on the Jeddah campus of King 'Abd al-'Aziz University following a discussion with a professor concerning a textbook that they perceived as insulting to Shi'i beliefs.[2] In September 1992, the Saudi authorities beheaded a Shi'i in Qatif whom the Interior Ministry had accused of renouncing Islam and blaspheming against God, the prophet Muhammad, and the Qur'an. This execution was apparently the first of its kind in modern Saudi Arabia.[3]

Much of the Saudi Shi'i opposition was broken and in exile during the Persian Gulf War, although its members had founded an organization in the 1980s, the *Munazzamat al-Thawra al-Islamiyya* (Organization of the Islamic Revolution) and had published a magazine, *al-Thawra al-Islamiyya,* from 1980 to 1991. Discourse between the Saudi regime and its Shi'i population evolved from confrontation in the 1980s to a search for cultural authenticity or a more creative form of resistance in the 1990s. This shift involved recognition of the limitations of confrontation and therefore sought to replace it with an assertion of Shi'i identity and demands for social equality.

To this end, the Shi'i organization changed its name to *al-Haraka al-Islahiyya* (the Reform Movement), and in 1991 it began to publish *al-Jazira al-'Arabiyya* in London and *Arabian Monitor* in Washington. These journals were moderate in tone and tended to highlight human rights abuses. They called for a progressive agenda in the kingdom and addressed issues other than those belonging to the Shi'a. Until the Committee for the Defense of Legitimate Rights (CDLR) began publishing in 1994, the Shi'a were the only overseas voice of the Saudi opposition.

The Shi'i Opposition Strikes

On June 25, 1996, a massive bomb destroyed much of the al-Khobar Towers housing complex in Dhahran, which housed U.S. Air Force personnel from the 4404th Fighter Wing (Provisional) and troops from the United Kingdom and France enforcing the United Nations–sponsored "no-fly zone" in southern Iraq. All nineteen people killed in the explosion were U.S. servicemen, and almost five hundred U.S. and other personnel were injured. The Council of Senior 'Ulama condemned the bombing as contrary to Islam. Even if most of the victims were non-Muslims, said the council, anyone who murders a non-Muslim who is under the protection of Muslims is guilty of "one of the greatest of all sins, the consequence of which is the denial of heaven."[4]

Three groups claimed credit for the attack. The first, which placed a telephone call to an Arabic-language newspaper in London, was the previously unknown "Legion of the Martyr 'Abdallah al-Hudayf." Al-Hudayf was the Saudi executed in 1995 for assaulting and maiming a Saudi security agent. In this communication, the al-Hudayf group claimed credit for the Riyadh blast as well, and it threatened further attacks if the United States did not remove its troops from the country. The second group to claim credit was "Hizballah–Gulf," also previously unknown. Its announcement was the first indication of a possible Iranian or Shi'i connection to the bombing. Claiming responsibility in a statement dated July 16 was the third group, the *Harakat al-Taghyir al-Islamiyya, al-Janah al-Jihadi fil-Jazira al-'Arabiyya* (Islamic Change Movement, the Jihad Wing in the Arabian Peninsula), an organization that had also claimed credit for the Riyadh bombing of 1995.[5]

As Saudi and U.S. investigators began to piece together the puzzle, they recalled several incidents that, in hindsight, may have presaged the violence. Following the November 1995 bombing in Riyadh, the U.S. embassy received threats of further violence should those arrested for the Riyadh bombing be executed. These threats included "crude drawings" that U.S. sources said could be interpreted as bomb threats against U.S. installations.[6] In addition, the U.S. investigation revealed that, in November 1995 and in January, March, April, and May 1996, U.S. Air Force security personnel at the complex reported that individuals were taking pictures and observing the compound through binoculars. On one occasion, a car bumped and moved one of the security barriers, apparently in an attempt to test the perimeter's strength as well as the readiness of U.S. security personnel.[7]

There were other signs of preparations for violence as well. On March 29, 1996, Saudi customs officials at the al-Haditha border checkpoint with Jordan arrested the driver of a car carrying an estimated thirty-eight kilograms of explosives and 116 meters of detonation cord. The car had traveled from Lebanon's Syrian-controlled Biqa' Valley. Saudi authorities arrested several others on the basis of their interrogation of the Saudi Shi'i driver.[8] Because the automobile had originated in the Biqa', U.S. officials privately linked Syria to the explosion, saying that U.S. investigators had identified individuals who had passed through Syria and had conducted surveillance of several U.S. military housing sites in the kingdom. In response, however, Prince Bandar bin Sultan, Saudi Arabia's ambassador to the United States, said Syria was "definitely not" connected to the bombing.[9]

The Saudis were slow in providing information, which caused serious tensions in Saudi–U.S. relations. The results of the investigation began to indicate Iranian involvement, although they did not rule out a Syrian connection as well. Then–U.S. secretary of defense William Perry told the Senate Armed Services Committee on July 9, 1996, that "an experienced and well-financed international terrorist organization" appeared to have provided support to the perpetrators. Given the sophistication and the size of the bomb, noted other Pentagon officials anonymously, it was becoming clear that a group outside the kingdom, or perhaps a foreign government, was behind the explosion, leading U.S. officials to investigate ties to Iraq or Iran. "If we identify another nation as the source of the bombing," said Perry, "we should retaliate."[10]

In early August 1996, Perry was more explicit. Asked if the Saudis had found a link to international terrorists, Perry said he anticipated that "there will be an international connection, yes." He added that Iran was "possibly" responsible and that the "general terms" of retaliation had been discussed with France and Britain.[11] The implied origin for these international terrorists was Hizballah. Perry was probably speaking about a series of arrests in the kingdom's Eastern Province, first reported on August 5. The London daily *al-Quds al-'Arabi*, one of the few international Arabic-language sources not controlled by Saudi Arabia, quoted a "reliable source" stating that three hundred Shi'is had been arrested. Those arrested were from a branch of the Shi'i opposition dissatisfied with an accommodation reached by Tawfiq al-Shaykh's group and the Saudi government in 1993 (see chapter 7). The accommodation was supposed to have eased restrictions on Shi'i activity and allow Shi'is to receive important government positions, this group claimed, but it had apparently failed.[12] Additionally, Israeli sources were quite certain of a Hizballah connection.[13] Coterminous reports also noted the arrest in the kingdom of six Sunnis, Saudi "Afghans" from the city of al-Khobar. According to an anonymous Saudi source, authorities linked some of the men arrested to the November 1995 Riyadh bombing as well.[14]

Arab and Western officials monitoring Hizballah-run training camps in Lebanon's Biqa' Valley noted that the region hosted numerous terrorist organizations—both Shi'i and Sunni—from Bahrain, Algeria, Egypt, and Saudi Arabia. In mid-August 1996, Saudi intelligence reportedly had found an electronic detonator in Dhahran of the type used by Hizballah and had discovered a video tape apparently showing Saudis undergoing training in eastern Lebanon. According to the report, Saudi authorities stopped four Saudis—not just one, as originally reported—at the al-Haditha crossing on March 29, "some" of whom were Shi'is.[15] In late August, reports surfaced that Iranian and Saudi technicians involved in the June 25 bombing had carried Syrian passports and that weapons transported to Saudi Arabia from Lebanon and Syria bore markings and serial numbers of military stockpiles in those two countries.[16]

In early September, Shi'i activists in Saudi Arabia went public with accusations that Saudi authorities were arresting their compatriots. The *Tajammu' 'Ulama al-Hijaz* (Hijazi 'Ulama Group) protested the arrest of Hujat al-Islam Hashim Muhammad al-Shakhsi, a Shi'i *'alim* (cleric) from al-Hasa, and listed the names of twenty-three other Shi'i clerics who had recently been arrested. Another group, the Committee for the Defense of Human Rights in the Hijaz, issued a similar announcement.[17] At the same time, the Movement for Islamic Reform in Arabia (MIRA) and an unnamed Saudi official stated that several Sunnis had been arrested for the blast.[18]

Saudi Arabia never officially announced any arrests for the Dhahran bombing, but reports on the detentions and confessions of Shi'is connected to Iran continued to proliferate. In mid-September, reliable diplomatic sources confirmed the incarcerations and reported that Syrian authorities had acceded to a Saudi request to arrest Ja'far al-Marzuq al-Shuwaykhat, a Saudi Shi'i living in Syria. When the Saudis arrived to take him into custody, the Syrians told them that al-Shuwaykhat had committed suicide in his cell. The Saudis had not publicly linked any detainees to Iran; speculation on this omission centered on the Saudi fear of repercussions that might stem from a U.S. retaliatory move against Iran.[19]

Many of the detentions involved members of "Saudi Hizballah," which operated within the framework of the Hijazi 'Ulama Group. It was unclear, however, whether the arrests were linked specifically to the bombing or whether the bombing was simply an opportunity for the Saudi authorities to detain Shi'i dissidents. Shi'i leaders in Qatif said the group had become more active in 1993, as it rejected the accommodation by King Fahd with other Shi'i groups. They said Shaykh Ja'far al-Mubarak, the leader of Saudi Hizballah, was under arrest.[20] Saudi officials issued a "no comment" response to questions about the arrests.[21]

In early November, alleged Saudi Hizballah official Husayn bin Mubarak was reportedly in Lebanon's Biqa' Valley, where he received comrades who had fled Saudi Arabia via Iran.[22] In mid-November an embarrassed Saudi Arabian security delegation, whose purpose was to investigate the connection between the Lebanese and Saudi Hizballah, canceled a trip to Beirut after Mubarak's reception of his comrades became public knowledge.[23] At the same time, a Shi'i organization in the kingdom—Hizballah al-Hijaz—began to issue threats against U.S. and Saudi targets should any harm befall "Sunnis and Shi'is" detained by the authorities.[24] The Islamic Change Movement issued a similar threat at the end of the month. Saudi officials made a number of arrests that averted an attack in the kingdom.[25]

Following U.S. Federal Bureau of Investigation (FBI) complaints in November concerning the lack of Saudi cooperation, then–FBI director Louis Freeh flew to Riyadh. According to "sources familiar with the matter," Saudi officials gave Freeh confessions and signals intelligence demonstrating that Saudi Shi'is, trained in Lebanon with the support of the Iranian government, had carried out the

Dhahran bombing. In their confessions, the reported perpetrators stated that Iranian intelligence had recruited them
during a Shi'i religious celebration in Damascus.[26]

Particularly noticeable in all reports was the lack of official Saudi comment. Interior Minister Prince Nayif bin 'Abd
al-'Aziz said in mid-December that the results of the investigation "will not take long." He called on the public to reject
any statements on the bombing that did not emanate from
the kingdom.[27]

In January 1997, U.S. sources, reportedly relying on information given to them by the head of Saudi intelligence,
Prince Turki bin Faysal, revealed that a Saudi Shi'i, Ahmad
Mughassil, was the mastermind behind the bombing and that
he was believed to be in Iran.[28] In March, Canadian officials
in Ottawa arrested Hani 'Abd al-Rahim al-Sayigh, a Saudi Shi'i
from the Eastern Province town of Sayhat, on suspicion of
involvement in the al-Khobar attack. He had entered Canada
in mid-August 1996 and applied for refugee status. It is likely
that he had been under surveillance since that time, probably because of information that the U.S. and Saudi
governments provided. The Saudis and U.S. law enforcement
officials thought al-Sayigh was the driver of the getaway car.
The FBI publicly thanked the Saudis for their "vigilant actions" and "invaluable assistance leading to the identification
and location" of al-Sayigh.[29]

In interviews from his detention cell, al-Sayigh gave con-
flicting accounts of his whereabouts on the day of the bombing
and of his political affiliation. At one time he said he had
been in Syria but later declared he was in Iran. At first, he
stated that he was part of a "political movement that was asking for democracy in Saudi Arabia," but then he denied that
he was affiliated with those movements. Al-Sayigh stated that
he feared returning to Saudi Arabia because it persecuted its
Shi'i minority.[30] There was also evidence that he had had contact with the Iranian Embassy in Ottawa. His arrest
demonstrated that the United States was now inclined to accept the Saudi theory that Saudi Shi'is had carried out the
attack with Iranian help and that some of those arrested in

the kingdom were involved. Previously, the FBI, which had been prevented from having a central role in the investigation, had been skeptical of this theory.[31]

At the end of March, the Canadian Security and Intelligence Service (CSIS) presented the Canadian Federal Court with documentation supporting its view that al-Sayigh was a terrorist involved in the al-Khobar explosion. The version of these documents released to the public was a sanitized summary and appeared to be the result of covert surveillance and investigation by U.S., Canadian, and Saudi authorities. The CSIS stated that it had "reasonable grounds" to believe that al-Sayigh was "a member of Saudi Hizballah, also known as Hizballah al-Hijazi." Moreover, the CSIS maintained, al-Sayigh had been a "direct participant" in the al-Khobar Towers bombing, had conducted surveillance at the site, and was the driver of a car which "signaled the explosives-laden truck to enter the parking lot." The Canadians also officially named al-Shuwaykhat, the Saudi Shi'i who reportedly committed suicide in a Syrian prison, as a "conspirator" in the plot and Mughassil as the "mastermind" behind the bombing.

The CSIS documents, as well as material submitted by al-Sayigh to a Saudi publication, provide a broad picture of al-Sayigh's activities. Members of his family were active in the Saudi Shi'i opposition, and he had joined them in meetings and in publishing underground journals. During these activities, he met al-Shuwaykhat and Mughassil and traveled to Syria, where he propagandized among Saudi Shi'is on pilgrimage to the tomb of Zaynab. It was also revealed that al-Shuwaykhat was his neighbor in Saudi Arabia and that he had studied in Qom and made contact with Iranian intelligence, which provided him with a forged passport. On his refugee application he denied having been in Iran, but he admitted it later. He also admitted to having been at one time a member of Saudi Hizballah.[32]

Meanwhile, in April, U.S. and Saudi intelligence officials linked Brig. Ahmad Sharifi, a top official of Iran's Islamic Revolutionary Guard Corps, to al-Sayigh and the bomb attack.[33] One U.S. official said, "Iran was the organizing force behind it [the attack]," although another official was careful to note that the evidence did not "rise to the level [necessary] for criminal prosecution." U.S. secretary of defense William Cohen stated that the United States had no concrete evidence directly linking any country to the bombing.[34] Cohen's statement reflected a problem inherent in the investigation. If proof existed of Iranian involvement, the United States would be forced to retaliate. Such an attack would have to be justified both internationally and at home, which could only be accomplished by revealing hard evidence. Even if the Saudis had such evidence, they were not likely to release it to the FBI.

The Canadian court's decision in May to deport al-Sayigh to the United States or Saudi Arabia motivated the suspect to cooperate with U.S. authorities.[35] On June 13, 1997, a Washington, D.C., grand jury returned an indictment against al-Sayigh, accusing him of conspiracy to commit murder and participating in international terrorism, charges that carried a maximum sentence of life in prison. The indictment specifically accused al-Sayigh of conspiring to kill U.S. nationals residing in Saudi Arabia. As part of the conspiracy, he was said to have traveled to the kingdom's Jizan region around December 1995 to purchase weapons on behalf of a terrorist organization.[36] No details of the terrorist organization or of the abortive attack have ever been released, because they remain part of a secret plea bargain.

The indictment, which made no mention of al-Khobar, was part of the plea bargain between the United States and al-Sayigh. He agreed to be deported to the United States (instead of Saudi Arabia) and stand trial on these charges, in exchange for providing information on the al-Khobar bombing. Al-Sayigh soon began to renege on the agreement, stating, according to his attorney, that he feared the information he provided would be used as the basis for retaliation again Iran and that in fact he had no knowledge of the al-Khobar bombing. On July 31, al-Sayigh entered a plea of not guilty and applied for political asylum in the United States. With the collapse of the plea arrangement, it became clear that the United States believed it did not have enough evidence to convict al-Sayigh on either the abortive 1995 attack or the al-Khobar bombing. The Justice Department dropped all charges against al-Sayigh and said it would consider extraditing him to Saudi Arabia, if the Saudis requested it and could provide an "adequate evidentiary showing."[37] At first, the Saudis did not comment officially on al-Sayigh, although an Interior Ministry official stated anonymously that al-Sayigh should be brought to the kingdom for questioning.[38] Interior Minister Prince Nayif later indicated that the Saudis had officially asked for his deportation, because al-Sayigh was "connected with a judicial case."[39]

On January 22, 1998, the U.S. Immigration and Naturalization Service (INS) issued a deportation order against al-Sayigh. This may have been a last-ditch effort by the FBI to force al-Sayigh to put his initial confession back on record. Although there was no room for appeal, al-Sayigh tried to find a country other that Saudi Arabia to take him, since he feared torture and execution there.[40] In early October 1999, the FBI put on the pressure again. Administration officials told the *Washington Post* that al-Sayigh had been informed that he would be sent to the kingdom immediately if he did not cooperate with U.S. investigators. The Justice Department said that the Saudis had said that they had "a basis" for prosecuting al-Sayigh and assured the United States that he would not be tortured.[41] Al-Sayigh's efforts to block his deportation failed, and he was returned to the kingdom in mid-October.[42] Interior Minister Prince Nayif stated that the Saudi government had "specific evidence and information that confirm the involvement of al-Sayigh in the unjust terrorist act . . . about three years ago."[43]

Such evidence may have been sufficient in Saudi Arabia, but apparently it was not enough for the U.S. courts to convict al-Sayigh. The Saudis may have also withheld such evidence to force al-Sayigh's extradition. Meanwhile, at the same time as the al-Sayigh episode, the U.S. investigation into the Dhahran attack had continued. In June 1997, a Saudi official stated that twelve Shi'is, including Ahmad Mughassil, were under suspicion for the bombing and were hiding in

Afghanistan and Lebanon. Some believed that all the suspects received training in Iran, but there were no direct links to the Iranian government. Significantly, the official elegantly let the Iranian government off the hook: "We believe," he stated, that *"rogue elements* in Iran financed and trained these men, probably without the knowledge or approval of the authorities [author's emphasis]."[44] It was evident that Riyadh was intent on solving the problem of Iranian subversion quietly, a decision that meshed nicely with a new Saudi policy of a rapprochement with Tehran.[45]

It was more comfortable for the Saudis to point to the Shi'i opposition as the source of the bombing, because the Shi'i minority is rather despised by the majority Sunnis. Previous years had witnessed a dramatic upsurge in Sunni opposition; blaming the Shi'is deflected attention from the potentially more threatening Sunni radicals. Indeed, according to MIRA, the real culprits in the al-Khobar bombing were actually seven Saudi Sunnis trained in Afghanistan, and they were being held by the Saudis.[46]

The Saudi rapprochement with Iran was now dictating Riyadh's policy in the bombing investigation. Relations had been improving steadily since 1996, and had grown closer since the election of President Khatami in May 1997. The Saudis reached an understanding with Iran to avoid providing the FBI with evidence of Iranian involvement in the al-Khobar bombing. U.S. sources said the evidence of Iranian participation, including U.S. intercepts of Iranian communications and detailed accounts from some participants detained in Saudi prisons, was overwhelming.[47] But the Saudis themselves could not produce a coherent communications strategy. They continued to announce that the investigation was over, or nearly over. In November 1997, Prince Nayif said, "The Saudi security services have the truth, but there are details of the investigation which have to be completed. . . . Once the details are all worked out, the results will be announced."[48] In March 1998, the minister announced that the investigation was complete, that "all the facts of this crime are with us . . . and we will leave the announcement for its time."[49] In

May, Prince Nayif said the bombing had been carried out by "Saudi hands . . . with support from others."[50] But the refusal of the Saudis to publicly confirm that the "others" were Iranians was, apparently, enough to close a deal with Iran. No details were available, but it seems likely that Riyadh agreed not to blame Iran publicly; in exchange, Tehran would agree not to support the activity of Saudi Shi'i oppositionists, and perhaps also help to locate such oppositionists hiding in Iran. Assertions in July 1998 by the son of a top Iranian official, Ahmad Rezai, that the attack was carried out by Hizballah–Gulf, based in Iran "with indirect support from the Iranian government," went largely unheeded.[51]

Although Prince Nayif announced in March 1998 that the investigation was complete and results would shortly be forthcoming, in March 1999 he said the government was still hoping to question people overseas.[52] A statement by State Department spokesman James Rubin in October 1999 that "we do have specific information with respect to the involvement of Iranian government officials" in the attack[53] seemed not to concern the Saudis. Saudi Arabia has yet to announce the results of the investigation; in light of the honeymoon in its current relations with Iran, it is unlikely that it will do so in the near future.[54]

Notes

1. See Jacob Goldberg, "The Shi'i Minority in Saudi Arabia," in Juan Cole and Nikki Keddie, eds., *Shiism and Social Protest* (New Haven, Conn.: Yale University Press, 1986), pp. 230–246 (analyzing Saudi Shi'i activity in the 1980s).

2. Aziz Abu-Hamad, "Empty Reforms: Saudi Arabia's New Basic Laws," *Middle East Watch*, New York, May 1992.

3. Caryle Murphy, "Saudi Beheading Draws Protests," *Washington Post*, October 1, 1992, p. A18.

4. See *al-Hayat*, July 1, 1996; *al-Yamama*, July 6, 1996.

5. Reuters, June 26, 1996; Reuters, June 27, 1996; *Times* (London), June 28, 1996; United Press International, July 19, 1996; Associated Press, July 19, 1996; Agence France-Presse, July 19, 1996; *al-Safir*, July 19, 1996; *al-Hayat*, July 20, 1996. The Movement for Islamic

Change's communication arrived at the office of *al-Hayat* just hours before the explosion of TWA flight 800 near New York on July 17, 1996. Although there was no proof connecting the group to that bombing, its statement noted eerily that "The invaders must be prepared to leave . . . Their time is at the dawn. Is not dawn near?"

6. Associated Press, "U.S. Warns Americans Living in Saudi Arabia," May 16, 1996; Douglas Jehl, "Saudis, Aided by the F.B.I., Seek Blast Clues," *New York Times*, June 27, 1996, p. A1; *Jerusalem Post*, May 22, 1996.

7. House National Security Committee, "Staff Report: The Khobar Towers Bombing Incident," August 14, 1996; Secretary of Defense, "Report to the President: Force Protection, Global Interest, Global Responsibilities," September 16, 1996.

8. SPA, April 18, 1996. See also *al-Yamama*, April 20, 1996 (containing pictures indicating how the explosives were stowed in the car).

9. R. Jeffrey Smith, "Syrian Link Probed in Saudi Blast," *Washington Post*, July 3, 1996, p. A1; Bill McAllister, "Syria Not Involved in 2 Attacks, Saudi Says," *Washington Post*, July 8, 1996, p. A12; *al-Hayat*, July 8, 1996; *al-Sharq al-Awsat*, July 8, 1996.

10. Philip Shenon, "Saudi Bombers Got Outside Support, Perry Tells Panel," *New York Times*, July 10, 1996, p. A1.

11. *International Herald Tribune*, August 3, 1996; *International Herald Tribune*, August 4, 1996.

12. See *al-Quds al-'Arabi*, August 5, 1996. See Chapter 7 for details of this accomodation.

13. *Ma'ariv*, August 13, 1996; *al-Hayat*, August 13, 1996.

14. See *al-Quds al-'Arabi*, August 10, 1996; *al-Quds al-'Arabi*, August 11, 1996; Youssef Ibrahim, "Local Militants Suspected in Dhahran Bomb," *International Herald Tribune*, August 15, 1996.

15. Edward Cody, "Trails of Many Muslim Fighters Mingle in Lebanon," *Washington Post*, August 18, 1996, p. A26.

16. Hillel Kuttler, "Report: Participants in Dhahran Bombing Carried Syrian Passports," *Jerusalem Post*, August 27, 1996, p. 2.

17. Reuters, September 13, 1996; "Riyadh Accused of Detaining Shiite Clerics as Sunnite Dissident Calls for Jihad Against U.S. Troops," *Mideast Mirror* 10, no. 172, September 4, 1996; *al-Quds al-'Arabi*, September 5, 1996; Compass News Service, September 9, 1996; Compass News Service , September 17, 1996.

18. "Riyadh Accused of Detaining Shiite Clerics as Sunnite Dissident Calls

for Jihad Against U.S. Troops," *Mideast Mirror* 10, no. 172, September 4, 1996; *Mideast Mirror*, September 18, 1996; *al-Quds al-'Arabi*, September 18, 1996.

19. "Al-Khobar Bombing Attributed to Iran-linked Saudi Shiites," *Mideast Mirror* 10, no. 182, September 18, 1996; *al-Quds al-'Arabi*, September 18, 1996.

20. *New York Times*, August 31, 1996; R. Jeffrey Smith, "Riyadh Holds 40 Saudis in Bombing," *International Herald Tribune*, November 2, 1996; *International Herald Tribune*, November 3, 1996.

21. See *al-Hayat*, October 28, 1996.

22. Radio Monte Carlo, November 4, 1996.

23. Compass, November 13, 1996.

24. Agence France-Presse, November 15, 1996, in "'First Statement' by al-Hijaz Warns Against Harming Detainees ," FBIS-NES-96-223 (online), November 19, 1996. Hizballah al-Hijaz is a violent movement founded in 1987 by Saudi Shi'i students in Najaf, who modelled themselves on the Lebanese Hizballah. It published *al-Fath* and *Risalat al-Haramayn*. *al-Jazira al-'Arabiyya*, July 1992.

25. Associated Press, "Militants Threaten G.I.s in Saudi Arabia," November 26, 1996; Reuters, November 28, 1996 (quoting U.S. secretary of defense William Perry).

26. Reuters, December 6, 1996; Reuters, December 11, 1996.

27. See *al-Sharq al-Awsat*, December 17, 1996;Radio Riyadh, December 17, 1996, in "Minister—'Not Much Longer' Until Blast Probe Announcement," FBIS-NES-96-243 (online), December 19, 1996.

28. David Makovsky, "U.S. Fingers Dhahran Bombing Suspect," *Jerusalem Post*, January 21, 1997, p. 1. The Saudis remain convinced of Mughassil's culpability. *Wall Street Journal*, May 26, 1999.

29. *Toronto Globe and Mail*, March 24, 1997.

30. Reuters, March 22, 1997; Reuters, March 23, 1997; Pierre Thomas and R. Jeffrey Smith, "Saudi Suspect May Be Driver in Bomb Plot," *Washington Post*, March 24, 1997, p. A01; Howard Schneider, "Jailed Saudi Denies Role In Bombing," *Washington Post*, March 25, 1997, p. A12; *New York Times*, March 25, 1997; *Ottawa Citizen*, March 23, 1997; *Toronto Globe and Mail*, March 25, 1997.

31. *New York Times*, March 25, 1997.

32. See CSIS document in Canadian Federal Court File No. DES-1-97. See Reuters, March 27, 1997; Anthony DePalma, "Canada Links Pro

Iranian Group To Saudi Attack at U.S. Barracks," *New York Times,* March 28, 1997, p. A1; Associated Press, March 28, 1997; Craig Turner and Robin Wright, "Hezbollah Support Network in Canada Alleged," *Los Angeles Times,* March 29, 1997, p. A6; Howard Schneider, "Suspect in Dhahran Bombing Describes Persecution of Saudi Shiites," *Washington Post,* March 29, 1997, p. A12; *Newsday,* March 29, 1997; Anthony DePalma, "Saudi Detained by Canadians Reveals Link to Blast Suspect," *New York Times,* March 29, 1997, sec. 1, p. 5; Agence France-Presse, March 29, 1997; *International Herald Tribune,* March 30, 1997. See also *al-Majalla,* April 20–29, 1997; Reuters, April 5, 1997. The covert surveillance revealed telephone calls between al-Sayigh and his family in Saudi Arabia, calls to Iran with conversation in Persian, and reference by al-Sayigh, in one call to some of his friends, that he was in "the country of Rafsanjani." *New York Times,* March 25, 1997.

33. Members of Bahraini Hizballah named Sharifi, alias Abu Jalal, as having recruited them while studying in Qom. Agence France-Presse, June 5, 1996; *al-Watan al-'Arabi,* May 13, 1997; *al-Watan al-'Arabi,* July 4, 1997.

34. Reuters, April 12, 1997; Reuters, April 21, 1997.

35. Reuters, May 5, 1997; Reuters, May 14, 1997; Pierre Thomas and David B. Ottaway, "Khobar Bombing Suspect May Cooperate With U.S.," *Washington Post,* May 17, 1997, p. A18; David Johnston, "Saudi Suspect In Canada Hints at Deal With the U.S.," *New York Times,* May 18, 1997, sec. 1, p. 4.

36. U.S. District Court for District of Columbia, Crim. No. 97-0251, *U.S.A v. Hani El-Sayegh,* filed June 13, 1997; Pierre Thomas, "Saudi Suspect May Cooperate In Bomb Probe," *Washington Post,* June 17, 1997, p. A10; Pierre Thomas and David B. Ottaway, "Saudi Bombing Suspect Arrives in Washington," *Washington Post,* June 18, 1997, p. A20; Associated Press, June 17, 1997.

37. Reuters, June 27, 1997; *New York Times,* July 7, 1997; Reuters, July 31, 1997; Toni Locy, "Saudi Ends Cooperation in Khobar Probe," *Washington Post,* July 31, 1997, p. A01; *International Herald Tribune,* September 9, 1997; Department of Justice, press release, September 8, 1997, online at http://www.usdoj.gov.

38. Associated Press, March 31, 1997.

39. *Gulf States Newsletter,* October 6, 1997.

40. *Middle East International,* February 27, 1998.

41. John Lancaster and David Vise, "Khobar Probe Figure Facing Deportation," Washington Post, October 5, 1999, p. A10.

42. Associated Press, October 6, 8,11 1999; Agence France-Presse, October 11, 1999.

43. Associated Press, October 11, 1999.

44. Associated Press, June 30, 1997 (author's emphasis).

45. For detailed discussions of the rapprochement, see Joshua Teitelbaum, "Saudi Arabia," in Bruce Maddy-Weitzman, ed., *Middle East Contemporary Survey (MECS) 1996*, (Boulder, Colo.: Westview, 1998), pp. 593–594; Joshua Teitelbaum, "Saudi Arabia," in Bruce Maddy-Weitzman, ed., *MECS 1997*, (Boulder, Colo.: Westview, 1999), pp. 618–620.

46. MIRA communiqué, February 1997, online at http://www.miraserve.com.

47. Online at http://www.abcnews.com, May 27, 1998.

48. Agence France-Presse, November 24, 1997.

49. Associated Press, March 30, 1998.

50. See *al-Qabas*, May 22, 1998; *al-Jazira*, June 1, 1998.

51. Agence France-Presse, July 15, 1998. Patrick Clawson has asserted that the Saudi reluctance to accuse Iran publicly was influenced by the appearance the United States gave of not intending to retaliate against Iran. Washington Institute *PolicyWatch*, no. 323, June 24, 1998).

52. Patrick Clawson, *PolicyWatch* no. 323, June 24, 1998; Agence France-Presse, October 21, 1998.

53. Online at http://www.abcnews.com, October 5, 1999.

54. In the context of seeking an opening to Iran, President Clinton approached Khatami in a secret letter in August 1999, asking for help in arresting three Saudi Shi'i members of Saudi Hizballah believed to have information about the Khobar Towers bombing, and were residing in Iran. Iran rejected the U.S. request. See *Mideast Mirror*, September 10, 1999; John Lancaster and Roberto Suro, "Clinton Reaches Out to Iran," *Washington Post*, September 29, 1999, p. A2; Afshin Molavi, "Iran Rejects U.S. Request for Help in Bombing Investigation," *Washington Post*, October 7, 1999, p. A30; Jane Perlez and James Risen, "Clinton Seeks an Opening to Iran, but Efforts Have Been Rebuffed," *New York Times*, December 3, 1999.

Chapter 7

Containing the Opposition:
The Al Sa'ud's Struggle with Dissent

D ifferent types of opposition, one mainstream Sunni and the other minority Shi'i, necessitated different Saudi containment policies. The radical Sunni fundamentalist opposition has always been the most difficult group for the Saudi regime to confront because it challenges the very foundation of the state, which claims a monopoly on Islam. The regime's first step in blunting the effect of the opposition was the introduction of institutions that give the impression of more participation in decision making. When this gambit failed, the regime attempted to coopt the opposition and further coopt the establishment *'ulama* (clerics) to shore up its legitimacy. With the Shi'is, it sought to placate and lower tension, so it could devote its efforts to combatting the more challenging Sunni opposition.

Creating a Majlis al-Shura

In November 1990, as dissent grew, King Fahd announced that he would soon create a *majlis al-shura* (Consultative Council), as well as a Basic Law of Government and a law for the provinces.[1] Never comprehending the intrinsic value of consultative institutions, the Saudi government had nevertheless often responded to pressure to share in the decision-making process by promising the establishment of a consultative council; the regime based its decision on the belief that Islam, while not condoning democracy, did allow for consultation. For example, after the capture of the Hijaz region, in 1926 Ibn Sa'ud announced the establishment of a council to coopt the local Hijazi leadership. Similar promises were made in 1932 and 1962, but

99

the institution existed only on paper. In March 1980—following the November 1979 occupation of the Meccan *haram* and disturbances in the Shi'i Eastern Province in December 1979 and February 1980—then–Crown Prince Fahd once again announced that he would establish a council, a law for the provinces, and a basic statute of government. Interior Minister Prince Nayif bin 'Abd Al-Aziz led the committee to draw up the laws,[2] but nothing came into being. Considering this history, King Fahd's 1990 announcement was greeted by many observers with a great deal of skepticism.

Nevertheless, in March 1992, the Consultative Council was officially created, and sixty members were appointed in August 1993; the council expanded to ninety in July 1997. The council does not have legislative powers but serves as a forum for discussion, even though these debates are held *in camera.* Moreover, although the council refuses membership to any radical fundamentalists, several establishment 'ulama are members, most prominently the chairman, Shaykh Muhammad bin Jubayr. About 19 percent of the 1993 council could be considered religious conservatives, compared with 17 percent of the expanded 1997 council.[3]

Apparently, the regime did try in 1997 to coopt some of the radical fundamentalists into the council. The London-based *al-Quds al-'Arabi,* which has close ties to Saudi opposition sources, noted that among the new members of the 1997 council were three men—Ahmad 'Uthman al-Tuwayjri, Mani' al-Juhani, and Zayd bin 'Abd al-Muhsin al-Husayn—closely associated with the two radical Sunni clerics, Salman bin Fahd al-'Awda and Safar bin 'Abd al-Rahman al-Hawali, who had themselves been jailed for expressing hard-line radical fundamentalist views. The paper identified three other members as "moderate Salafis."[4]

Three Shi'is were named to the 1997 council to join one originally appointed to the 1993 council. The additions may have been intended to appease the country's Shi'is, who were generally upset about their situation, their lack of representation, and the arrests of 1996 that followed the bombing of the U.S. barracks in Dhahran. The four Shi'i members on the ninety-seat council were intended to represent the 13 percent figure often touted as the percentage of Shi'is in the kingdom.[5]

Placating the Opposition with Increased Spending

In financial matters, the radical Sunni fundamentalist opposition had stressed in its 1991 petition that unfair fees and taxes should be removed. To slow the growing strength of the opposition, in March 1992 King Fahd drastically reduced the prices of cooking gas, gasoline, electricity, and water by amounts ranging from 28.5 percent to 50 percent.[6] This decision contradicted all financial logic, because Saudi Arabia would likely accumulate a large budget deficit for the tenth consecutive year and was already one of the highest per capita water users in the world.[7] Financial considerations, however, were secondary to the desire of the regime to placate foes who called its Islamic legitimacy into question.

As a further sign of conciliation to the radical fundamentalist opposition, the Ministry of Pilgrimage and Religious Trusts announced in 1992 that the Saudi government had spent 3.2 billion Saudi riyals (about $853.1 million) in recent years on mosque construction, employed 54,000 religious functionaries in mosques, and planned to hire another 7,300 *imams* (prayer leaders) and *mu'adhdhins* (those who issue the call to prayer) in 1992 alone.[8] The government, nevertheless, was in the same seemingly no-win situation as other regimes facing an Islamic challenge. It could try to monopolize religion, manage the purse strings, and coopt the opposition, but in doing so it would run the risk of expanding the opposition's infrastructure—the mosque network itself.

Shoring Up Religious Support

In the face of mounting radical fundamentalist opposition, the regime moved to shore up religious support where it existed. In what appeared to be another effort to coopt leading religious figures, King Fahd announced in July 1993 that Shaykh 'Abd al-'Aziz bin Baz had been appointed General Mufti of Saudi Arabia, with the rank of minister—the first time the position had been filled since the death of the previous mufti in 1969. He was also named president of the Council of Senior 'Ulama and of the *Idarat al-Buhuth al-Islamiyya wal-Ifta* (Administration of Islamic Studies and Rulings). The former Ministry of Hajj and Pious Endowments Affairs was split into two ministries: a new *Shu'un Islamiyya wal-Awqaf wal-Da'wa wal-Irshad* (Ministry of Islamic Affairs, Pious Endowments, Mission, and Guidance), with Dr. 'Abdallah bin 'Abd al-Muhsin al-Turki, director of Imam Muhammad bin Sa'ud Islamic University, as its minister; and a Ministry of Hajj Affairs headed by Dr. Mahmud bin Muhammad Safar.[9]

Interpretations of the moves in the Saudi press and in interviews granted by the new appointees reflected the image the royal family wished to project. Creation of the new ministries, wrote the daily *al-Jazira*, proved that the decision-making process in the kingdom was based on *shura* (consultation).[10] Al-Turki said his new ministry was a renewed sign of the enormous support that the kingdom gives to Islam and its propagation.[11] A long profile of Bin Baz, published in *al-Majalla*, stressed that his most famous fatwa had prohibited the worship of relics, a practice that led to *shirk* (polytheism), or attributing holiness to objects and therefore detracting from the *tawhid* (oneness) of God; the Wahhabis defined many Shi'i practices similarly. It further noted that Bin Baz always called for obeying the rulers; theoretically, even if they were evil, evil could not be removed by a more evil thing. He also forbade the killing of unbelievers who had been permitted to enter the country by the state—a reference to Christians, and perhaps Jews, who visited or worked in the country. Of course, another of Bin Baz's fatwas may have been more memorable to many Saudis: his ruling in 1966 that the world was flat.[12]

These moves signified the increasing importance Fahd attached to legitimation by the religious establishment in the face of the radical fundamentalists' ongoing threat. Bin Baz was the leading *'alim* (cleric) in the country and was often needed to justify governmental actions. Al-Turki was head of the most important Islamic university, which produced several radical fundamentalist activists. Thus, two leading religious figures were now part of the government and would share responsibility for its actions.

The regime relied on Bin Baz for his legitimizing views. He told *al-Sharq al-Awsat* that Muslims must comply with the ruler as long as the ruler does not sin; if he does sin, one can fight him, but only if this does not lead to a greater evil, such as corruption, disrupting public order, or the killing of innocent people. Those who commit such acts, he said, even if their zeal is commendable, are sinning and will end up in hell.[13] Speaking at a graduation ceremony for forty-three preachers who had completed a Ministry of Islamic Affairs–sponsored program aimed at stressing Islam's more moderate teachings, Bin Baz attacked the radical Sunni fundamentalist Committee for the Defense of Legitimate Rights (CDLR) and said that those who really wanted reform should cooperate with the rulers and ask God to guide them.[14] Minister of Justice 'Abdallah bin Muhammad Al al-Shaykh told a Western interviewer that "even in religious matters the state is the final authority." He continued:

> It is forbidden in Islam to raise a hand against the ruler. If he makes a mistake—even a big one like corruption, and that includes adultery or stealing or drinking—overthrowing him is prohibited. If he forces others to violate Islam, you may refuse to follow him, but you can go no further. Overthrow of a ruler is not permitted, because when a people is without a ruler the result is *fitna*—public disorder—and that is worse than corrupt rule. Obedience to [a] ruler is part of Muslim practice.[15]

The regime also prevailed upon the highest ranking CDLR 'alim, 'Abdallah bin al-Jibrin, to repudiate his CDLR membership. Bin al-Jibrin's renouncement denied knowing CDLR members and condemned the way in which CDLR spokesman Muhammad al-Mas'ari had used the foreign press. He added that he was accustomed to interceding with the authorities and offering them advice, as had been the custom of the 'ulama, and he implied that this role was the CDLR's mission.[16]

The establishment 'ulama found it easiest to condemn
the overseas-based CDLR than the "Awakening Shaykhs" at
home. In what amounted to an admission that the
organization's faxes were widely distributed in the kingdom,
in November 1994 three prominent establishment 'ulama,
Bin Baz, Bin al-Jibrin, and Shaykh Muhammad bin Salih
al-'Uthaymin, condemned the CDLR faxes as seditious. Bin
Baz warned Saudis "not to read them or look at them. A Muslim . . . should not cause unrest but should try to unite people
with advice, guidance, and benign words." Al-'Uthaymin said
such publications were slanderous and that it was a sin to
slander rulers. Bin al-Jibrin issued a mild condemnation of
al-Mas'ari's faxes, which he said should not be distributed or
published "regardless if they are true or not." Most important to the regime, Bin Baz's and al-'Uthaymin's statements
supported the royal family and emphasized unity and respect
for authority.[17]

Probably the most severe condemnation of CDLR tactics
came from Shaykh Salih al-Luhaydan, a member of the Council of Senior 'Ulama and head of the *Majlis al-Qudat al-A'la*
(Higher Council of Qadis). He did not name names but stated,

> *Nasiha* [advice, admonition] has certain conditions, prin-
> ciples, and rules of its own. One who wants to say everything
> that comes to mind without acting according to the rules
> of the Islamic shari'a concerning *al-amr wal-nahy* [positive
> and negative commandments] is one or the other: either a
> *jahil* [ignoramus], who must be taught; or an *'alim* [man of
> knowledge], who has gone too far and therefore must be
> debated until he understands; if he remains obstinate, he
> must be restrained.

Noting that the nation must remain united, al-Luhaydan added
that "only the enemies of Islam profited from disunity."[18]

In addition to arranging support from establishment
'ulama, the government-controlled press initiated a smear
campaign against the Awakening Shaykhs. The weekly
al-Majalla accused them of abusing the tolerance of the kingdom and taking advantage of undeveloped young minds to

sow discord. "Is there any country in the world which implements the shari'a more than Saudi Arabia?" asked *al-Majalla* incredulously. The two shaykhs, it concluded, had "removed themselves [*kharaju 'an*] from the consensus of the community of believers [*'ijma al-umma*]."[19]

Protecting the Monopoly on Islam

As part of the regime's efforts to control Islamic discourse in the country and to maintain a monopoly on Wahhabi Islam as lived and interpreted in Saudi Arabia, the Saudi government stepped up its efforts to prepare preachers who would spread the "correct" version of Islam. Addressing a group of newly accredited preachers, Bin Baz accused CDLR founder Shaykh 'Abdallah bin Sulayman al-Mas'ari of attacking Muhammad bin 'Abd al-Wahhab as primitive and without knowledge. The true reforming preacher, according to Bin Baz, calls for Muslims to draw nearer to God, adhere to religion and advice, and cooperate with the rulers. "The correct preacher thanks [the rulers] for all the good and efforts they invest and warns against [people like al-Mas'ari]."[20]

Yet, the growing assertiveness of the establishment 'ulama, represented mostly by the Council of Senior 'Ulama headed by Bin Baz, worried the regime. For years, Riyadh had not been entirely confident of the council's loyalty, which seemed to be increasingly influenced by the radical Sunni fundamentalists' agenda. For example, the Saudi-sponsored Muslim World League (MWL) called on Muslims to "actively participate" in the 1994 United Nations (UN) conference on population and development, so as to express their objections.[21] Yet, the Council of Senior 'Ulama called the conference "an insult to Islam" and directed the Saudi government to boycott the meeting.[22] That pressure forced the regime to cancel its participation,[23] even though Saudi Arabia has one of the highest population growth rates in the world.

Indeed, the radical and establishment 'ulama shared similar educational experiences and held similar views. Thus, even after he agreed that al-Hawali and al-'Awda should be pre-

vented from speaking, Bin Baz issued a private fatwa to someone who inquired about the propriety of listening to the tapes
of the two shaykhs (as well as those of their colleagues, 'A'id
al-Qarni, Nasir al-'Umar, and 'Abd al-Wahhab al-Turayri). The
petitioner asked if the Awakening Shaykhs were *mubtada'a*
(innovators) or *khawarij* (deviationists), not *salafis* (loyalists
to the Islamic tradition). Bin Baz replied that they were worthy people and not innovators; they should be heard, even if
they made mistakes.[24]

Disappointed with the lack of a forceful response from the
Council of Senior 'Ulama to the September 1994 protests, King
Fahd announced in October the creation of the *al-Majlis al-A'la
lil-Shu'un al-Islamiyya* (Supreme Council of Islamic Affairs) in
an attempt to marginalize the 'ulama. Composed of Interior
Minister Prince Nayif, Foreign Minister Sa'ud Al Faysal, and
other ministers, and headed by Minister of Defense Prince
Sultan bin 'Abd al-'Aziz, it contained no 'ulama.[25] Although
the supreme council's official mandate was to help Muslims
abroad by establishing a general framework for Islamic affairs
headed by the royal family, the Saudis sought to take some of
the initiative away from the establishment 'ulama and the radical fundamentalists, both of which were demanding greater
activity in this area. A few days later, another body was formed,
the *al-Majlis lil-Da'wa wal-Irshad* (Council for Islamic Mission
and Guidance), chaired by Dr. 'Abdallah al-Turki,[26] minister
of Islamic affairs, religious endowments, mission, and guidance.
Although a member of the royal family did not lead this council, and its formation did not receive as much attention in the
press, it may actually have been more important than the Supreme Council of Islamic Affairs. The Council for Mission and
Guidance included several trusted establishment religious officials, such as the rector of the Imam Muhammad bin Sa'ud
Islamic University and the general president of the Committee for the Enjoining of Good and the Prevention of Evil
(known abroad as the kingdom's "religious police"). It was
charged with *da'wa* (in this case, propagating the "proper" version of Islam) within Saudi Arabia, which included the selection
of *du'at* (preachers), supervision of the contents of the mes-

sage, the selection and supervision of mosque functionaries, and the supervision of mosque activities.[27] The creation of both councils was defensive in nature: The radical Sunni fundamentalists occupied numerous positions in the universities and other religious institutions, and the councils were designed to supervise their activity more directly.

These bodies reportedly met in 1995, but their impact was difficult to measure. The Supreme Council for Islamic Affairs met at least twice during the year, but details about the meetings were mostly laconic and revealed little information, noting only that the council had discussed the situation of Muslims around the world and taken appropriate steps.[28] The Council for Islamic Mission and Guidance met at least once, but unlike reports from the other council, reports on this meeting were quite instructive. This council had as its goal the training, guiding, and supervision of the imams, *khatibs* (deliverers of the Friday sermon in the mosques), and du'at throughout the kingdom's entire mosque system, where the regime realized the battle for the hearts and minds of its citizens was taking place. In a speech to the Council for Islamic Mission and Guidance, al-Turki demonstrated the Saudi royal family's desire to buttress its Islamic legitimacy via the appropriation of the legacy of the founder of Wahhabism, Muhammad bin 'Abd al-Wahhab. Al-Turki held up the Al Sa'ud as the primary historical propagator of Bin 'Abd al-Wahhab's da'wa (creed) for *islah* (reform) and *tajdid* (renewal). The leader of the Al Sa'ud in each generation was the imam of those who followed Bin 'Abd al-Wahhab, he said. The Saudi royal family and thus the Saudi state was eternally charged with carrying forth the message of Wahhabism— *tawhid,* or the indivisible unity of God.[29]

It was on this claim that the battle with the radical fundamentalists was joined. The Al Sa'ud and its court 'ulama, the fundamentalists maintained, had long ago cast off the mantle of Bin 'Abd Al-Wahhab, which the Awakening Shaykhs had picked up. It was unlikely, therefore, that the creation of the councils, so manifestly self-serving, would placate the growing radical Sunni fundamentalist sentiment.

The formation of the Council for Islamic Mission and Guidance represented more of the centralizing, state-building effort that has characterized the Al Sa'ud. The royal family wished to have a monopoly on the da'wa of Bin 'Abd al-Wahhab: "to set the policy for da'wa" was the phrase used in official documents. The goal was to combat the radical fundamentalists, who represented traditional, tribal, and centrifugal tendencies, and who were resisting the state's attempts to monopolize Islam.[30]

The regime escalated the confrontation with the opposition by beheading one of its supporters, 'Abdallah bin 'Abd al-Rahman bin 'Abdallah al-Hudayf, a 33-year-old businessman, in August 1995, the first such execution in many years. Al-Hudayf was convicted of attempting to kill Maj. Sa'ud bin Shibrin, an officer of the *al-Mabahith al-'Amma* (Department of General Investigations), by throwing acid in his face. Nine other oppositionists were given tough prison sentences in the same trial, including two relatives of al-Hudayf. Two of those arrested were professors at King Sa'ud University. The Interior Ministry specifically accused Muhammad al-Mas'ari of giving instructions to the perpetrators. According to an official statement, the group had cached arms and was planning violent activities against the government, after which they had planned to leave the country with the help of al-Mas'ari's connections.[31] The official statement on the al-Hudayf execution stressed that those sentenced has supported a faction—the CDLR—which had *kharajat* (withdrawn) from the obligation to listen and obey the *wali al-amr* (legitimate ruler) and the 'ulama who had issued a fatwa proclaiming the illegitimacy of the CDLR. Although the regime had previously complained about the CDLR, mostly through its 'ulama, this episode marked the first time that a public connection had been drawn between the CDLR and active subversion. That the execution was carried out in secret may have been a signal that the regime feared popular reaction.

Accommodating the Shi'i Opposition

The Shi'i opposition tried to open avenues of communication with some of the Sunni opposition during the 1990s, but, as could perhaps be expected, they were rebuffed. The Saudi regime noticed and welcomed the shift in Shi'i tactics and apparent goals, for it faced a more radical and more threatening Sunni opposition. Following negotiations carried out by the Saudi ambassador to the United Kingdom, Ghazi al-Qusaybi, several members of the Shi'i opposition returned to Saudi Arabia in the autumn of 1993.[32]

For the Saudi government, accommodating the Shi'i opposition seemed a relatively easy way to temper a serious conflict, even at the cost of angering radical Sunni fundamentalists at home. Saudis already owned most of the international Arab press, and for a small price they could shut down two major opposition publications. Moreover, the Shi'i group appeared to have settled for a separate deal with the Saudis, accepting commitments to improve the situation of the Eastern Province Shi'is and agreeing not to press their demands for general reform and human rights domestically. Compared to the tougher and potentially more dangerous demands of groups such as the CDLR, reaching a separate *modus vivendi* with the Shi'i opposition was a small price to pay and also prevented a temporary but potentially damaging alliance between the opposition movements.

Tawfiq al-Shaykh, a leader of the Saudi Shi'i opposition in exile, led a large delegation to Saudi Arabia in October 1993 to meet with King Fahd and other Saudi officials. According to the few press reports available, Fahd instructed Prince Muhammad bin Fahd, governor of the Eastern Province, to carry out Shi'i demands, which included allowing the practice of Shi'i religious rites previously outlawed, returning cancelled passports, allowing exiles to return, and guaranteeing that those who returned would not be arrested or questioned. As a result of these contacts, the authorities released scores of Shi'i prisoners and issued travel documents previously denied to Shi'i activists. In a development the Shi'is perceived as highly significant, the Saudi regime reportedly reissued a school text that had referred to Shi'is as one of the heterodox sects. The new edition mentioned that there were now five Islamic *madhahib* (schools of jurisprudence) in Saudi

Arabia: four belonging to *Ahl al-Sunna wal-Jama'a* (Sunnis) and one belonging to the *imamiyya* or *ithna 'ashariyya* (Shi'is). The Shi'i publications *al-Jazira al-'Arabiyya* and *Arabia Monitor* published their last issues in August 1993.

Both sides kept the news of the agreements fairly quiet;[33] the Saudi domestic and overseas press ignored it, and opposition activists suddenly assumed a very low profile. This reaction probably resulted from a mutual understanding that too much publicity would draw the fire of radical Sunni fundamentalists, who were troublesome for both the Al Sa'ud and the Shi'is.

Both the government and the Shi'i opposition seemed to have greatly desired some arrangement, although it appeared that the Saudi authorities emerged victorious, having successfully silenced several of its major critics. There was no evidence that certain other key Shi'i demands had been met, including the official recognition of Shi'ism as a Muslim *madhhab* (school of Islamic jurisprudence) and the right to implement Shi'i law accordingly; recognition of the rights to build and to worship in Shi'i holy places—*husayniyyat* (Shi'i meeting houses) and mosques—and to repair graves destroyed by the Saudis in the al-Baqi' cemetery in Medina; freedom to hold Shi'i religious celebrations; an end to discrimination against Shi'is in government and universities; and general improvements in the Eastern Province.[34] Additionally, not all Shi'is accepted the new accommodation with the regime, and some members of the overseas opposition did not return.

Notes

1. Jacob Goldberg, "Saudi Arabia," in Ami Ayalon, ed., *Middle East Contemporary Survey (MECS) 1990* (Boulder, Colo.: Westview, 1992), p. 620.

2. Jacob Goldberg, "Saudi Arabia," in C. Legum et al., eds., *MECS 1979–80* (New York: Holmes and Meier, 1981), pp. 694–695.

3. For the text of the law mandating the creation of the Consultative Council, see Joshua Teitelbaum, "Saudi Arabia," in Ami Ayalon, ed., *MECS 1992* (Boulder, Colo.: Westview, 1995), pp. 691–697. On the formation of the Consultative Council, see Joshua Teitelbaum, "Saudi Arabia," in Ami Ayalon, ed., *MECS 1993* (Boulder, Colo.: Westview,

1995), pp. 582–583; and R. Hrair Dekmejian, "Saudi Arabia's Consultative Council," *Middle East Journal* 55 (spring 1998), pp. 204–218.

4. *Al-Quds al-'Arabi,* July 8, 1997.

5. Reuters, July 6, 1997; *al-Hayat,* July 7, 1997; *al-Sharq al-Awsat,* July 7, 1997; "Saudi Shiites Quadruple Their Share in Expanded Shoura Council," *Mideast Mirror* 11, no. 129, July 7, 1997; *al-Wasat,* July 14, 1997. See also *al-Quds al-'Arabi,* July 8, 1997.

6. Saudi Press Agency (SPA), March 23, 1992; *Financial Times,* March 25, 1992.

7. *Wall Street Journal,* January 15–16, 1993.

8. *Economist Intelligence Unit, CountryReport: Saudi Arabia,* no. 1, 1992, p. 9.

9. *Financial Times,* July 12, 1993; *Le Monde,* July 13, 1993; *al-Hayat,* July 14, 1993. Turki was a member of the Council of Senior 'Ulama. Safar, born in Mecca in 1939, was a civil engineer educated at Stanford and the University of North Carolina, who had held several high academic positions , including the presidency of the Arabian Gulf University in Bahrain. His last position was professor in the Department of Engineering at the King Fahd University of Petroleum and Mines. See *al-Majalla,* July 25–31, 1993.

10. See *al-Jazira,* cited by SPA, July 12, 1993.

11. See *al-'Ukaz,* July 12, 1993.

12. See *al-Majalla,* July 25–31, 1993.

13. See *al-Sharq al-Awsat,* May 22, 1993.

14. United Press International, April 15, 1995.

15. Milton Viorst, "The Storm in the Citadel," *Foreign Affairs* (January/February 1996).

16. See *al-Hayat* (London), May 26, 1993; *al-Jazira al-'Arabiyya* (May , June 1993); Movement for Islamic Reform in Arabia (MIRA), *History of Dissent: The Story of Islamic Dissent in Arabia,* chapter 12, "Official Reactions to the Committee for the Defence of Rights," online at http://www.miraserve.com/chap12.html.

17. See *al-Hayat,* November 18, 1994 (quoting Al-'Uthaymin); *al-Hayat,* October 3, 1994 (quoting Jibrin); SPA, November 10—BBC, November 12, 1994 (quoting Bin Baz); BBC-SWB, November 12, 1994 (quoting Bin Baz); and Reuters, November 11, 1994 (quoting Bin Baz). The CDLR contended that Bin Baz had been blackmailed into

condemning it because Interior Minister Nayif had promised "the naive Shaykh" that he would release prisoners if Bin Baz condemned the CDLR. *CDLR Monitor,* no. 23, November 25, 1994.

18. See *al-Hayat,* October 3, 1994.

19. See *al-Majalla,* October 9–15, 1994.

20. Ibid.; *al-Riyadh,* April 15, 1995.

21. *Arab News,* August 17, 1994.

22. Youssef M. Ibrahim, "Saudi King Trying to Dilute Islamic Radicalism," *New York Times,* October 6, 1994, p. A5.

23. See *al-Hayat,* August 30, 1994; *Financial Times,* August 30, 1994; Michael Georgy, "Saudis Snub Population Talks as Insult to Islam," *International Herald Tribune,* August 30, 1994.

24. Al-Rifa'i, *Al-Mashru' al-Islahi fi al-Sa'udiyya,* pp. 178–179 (citing the *fatwa* of Bin Baz).

25. See *al-Hayat,* October 5, 1994.

26. In an interesting commentary, perhaps demonstrating the cooptation of certain Islamist trends, MSANEWS noted with respect to Turki that he belonged to the "underground" leadership of the Saudi Muslim Brethren, but that he was loyal to the royal family and therefore "at odds with the more salafist trend striving to strip the Saudi family of any legitimacy." MSANEWS, October 9, 1994.

27. See *al-Sharq al-Awsat,* October 9, 1994.

28. See *al-Hayat,* February 9, 1994; *al-Hayat,* August 2, 1994; *al-Sharq al-Awsat,* August 2, 1995.

29. See *al-Sharq al-Awsat,* May 27, 1995.

30. The goals of the council and its monopoly on *da'wa* are displayed on the council's website, at http://www.islam.org.sa/WAZARA/WAZARA_R62_E.htm. Even the domain name, www.islam.org.sa, reserved exclusively for the use of the Islamic Affairs Ministry, suggests its monopoly on Islam and da'wa. Since 1999, Saudi Arabia's Islamic institutions have realized the necessity of joining battle with the radical fundamentalists on the internet, where the latter have had a greater presence for many years.

31. See *al-Sharq al-Awsat,* August 13, 1995; *al-Hayat,* August 13, 1995; *al-Quds al-'Arabi,* August 15, 1995; "Saudi Arabia Executes an Islamist Opponent," Human Rights Watch/Middle East news release, August 17, 1995.

32. Madawi Al-Rasheed, "The Shi'a of Saudi Arabia: A Minority in Search of Cultural Authenticity," *British Journal of Middle Eastern Studies* 25 (1998), pp. 121–138; Mamoun Fandy, "From Confrontation to Creative Resistance," *Critique* (fall 1996), pp. 1–27; Joshua Teitelbaum, "Saudi Arabia," in Ami Ayalon, ed., *Middle East Contemporary Survey (MECS) 1993* (Boulder, Colo.: Westview, 1995), pp. 575–600; "What Future for the Saudi-Shiite Accord?," *Mideast Mirror* 8, no. 54, March 18, 1994.

33. See *al-Diyar*, October 13, 1993; Youssef M. Ibrahim, "Saudi Officials Reporting Accord with Shiite Foes," *New York Times*, October 29, 1993, p. A11; *al-Quds al-'Arabi*, November 1, 1993; *al-'Alam*, November 13, 1993; For Shi'i oppositionist attacks on the Saudi regime, see various issues of *al-Jazira al-'Arabiyya* and *Arabia Monitor*, as well as the article in the summer 1993 issue of the *Arab Review*, detailing Saudi abuse of holy sites in Mecca and Medina.

34. See *al-'Alam*, November 13, 1993.

Chapter 8

Conclusion: Saudi Arabia, the Opposition, and Crown Prince 'Abdallah

The growth of the post–1991 Gulf War radical fundamentalist movement represented both continuity and a departure for Saudi Arabia. The forces at work were the same centrifugal forces that have plagued the Saudi state since its creation. The radical fundamentalists opposed the Saudi version of the state, resented the monopoly of the ruling family, the Al Sa'ud, and wanted Islam decentralized into the hands of *'ulama* (clerics) of their own choosing—'ulama who were leaders by virtue of their stature among the faithful and not because they had been chosen by the Al Sa'ud. Although the Saudis had been successful for years in suppressing the decentralizing trend, the economic downturn that began in the 1980s created an opportunity for resentment to build once again. It exploded after the 1991 Gulf War, when the Saudi regime demonstrated that it could no longer defend the community of believers. The popularity of the "Awakening Shaykhs," the public petitions, the demonstrations, and the founding of the Committee for the Defense of Legitimate Rights (CDLR) were all evidence that the Islam of the Al Sa'ud was no longer legitimate to important sectors, and therefore its power as a legitimizing factor appeared limited.

The Al Sa'ud have created a massive array of Islamic institutions, from those issuing fatwas to those training preachers. Qur'ans are printed and distributed by the millions. Every year at the hajj and most recently on the Internet, the Al Sa'ud projects a persona of a benevolent family that furthers Islam and facilitates the attainment of religious obligations, with

115

the stated purpose of propagating the fundamentalist Islamic vision of Muhammad bin 'Abd al-Wahhab. Moreover, it can call on the establishment 'ulama to legitimize the family's right to rule.[1] It appears that many of the world's Muslims accept the Saudi royal family as the guardians of a true Islam.

Centralizing Islamic institutions was part of the Saudi process of state building. Islam became identified with the state, and religious functions became state functions. This arrangement appears to have worked smoothly, for the most part, in times of economic prosperity. But when the situation became worse, those who opposed this centralizing tendency began the radical Sunni fundamentalist movement. Leaders who once kept their thoughts to themselves were ready, for the first time, to point out publicly the contradiction between the Al Sa'ud's Islamic persona and what they saw as an entirely different reality. Further impetus for change was provided by the arrival of U.S. and other "unbelieving" troops, a development that demonstrated to the radicals that, despite years of military spending, King Fahd—he who would arrogate to himself the title of *imam* (religious leader) of those who followed the *da'wa* (creed) of Bin 'Abd al-Wahhab—could not defend the community of the faithful. Fahd could call himself Guardian of the Two Holy Shrines, but the real guardian was the U.S. Central Command (CENTCOM). The humiliation was too much for the radical fundamentalists to bear.

Saudi Arabia under 'Abdallah: Return to Faysal's Order?

Since November 1995, however, Crown Prince 'Abdallah bin 'Abd Al-'Aziz, deputy prime minister and commander of the Saudi Arabian National Guard (SANG), has been king of Saudi Arabia in all but name. Since then, radical fundamentalist activity has ebbed to its lowest point since the Persian Gulf War, even though the socioeconomic situation has seen ups and downs. The drop in oil prices yielded estimated 1998 earnings from petroleum exports of only $29.4 billion, down 35 percent from 1997, but the upswing in oil prices in 1999 brought in 17 percent more than in 1998. As a result, per capita gross domestic product (GDP) was up slightly in 1999, to around

$7,000—still a far cry from the oil boom years. But this was expected to improve in 2000 as oil prices continued to climb. A midyear report by the Saudi American Bank stated that 2000 would be strongest year for oil revenues since the peak of the oil boom in 1981. Even so, warned the report, revenues were no longer adequate to sustain growth and job creation. The population's growth rate in 1999 was still very high at 3.3 percent, compared with 0.91 percent in the United States and 0.40 percent in France. By 1999, the number of people in Saudi Arabia younger than 20 years of age had climbed to 52 percent of the population, compared with 29 percent in the United States and 26 percent in France. The population was still inordinately young, and there were few jobs available.[2]

Adjusting to Economic Realities

Since the mid-1990s, Saudi Arabia has made some adjustments to address these economic realities. In 1994 and 1995 the government cut the budget, mostly in wheat supports and subsidies for utilities and services, but presented the cuts as one-time measures.[3] In the 1999 budget, there were further signs of this emerging pragmatism when the government announced a hiring freeze and cut defense spending by 30 percent. It also increased the price of gasoline by 50 percent.[4]

The Supreme Economic Council, which was charged with increasing jobs for Saudi nationals, promoting the private sector, and boosting foreign investment, was also created in 1999. In January 2000, 'Abdallah announced the formation of yet another council, the Council for Petroleum and Mineral Affairs.[5] It is difficult at this stage to assess the impact of these bodies, but their formation may suggest that the regime realizes a pressing need for reform. All the same, there have been no serious structural changes in the economy. At times it seems as if the Saudis put their faith in windfall profits from a rise in oil prices. Indeed, a subsequent rise in oil prices in 2000 did not bring about any radical changes in Saudi economic policy.

Crown Prince 'Abdallah has told the Saudi people that things must change. At the annual Gulf Cooperation Council (GCC) summit in Abu Dhabi in December 1998, he

surprised those assembled by proclaiming that "the boom period is gone for good and . . . we have to become used to a
different lifestyle in which every individual should perform
their effective role and not totally rely on the state."[6]

A Realignment in Foreign Policy

Many in Saudi Arabia have high hopes for Crown Prince
'Abdallah. He has distanced himself from King Fahd's anti-
Iran policy and initiated an unparalleled honeymoon period
between Riyadh and Tehran. During Iranian president
Muhammad Khatami's landmark visit to Saudi Arabia in May
1999, 'Abdallah announced the appointment of a Shi'i as
Saudi ambassador to Tehran. In July 2000, both Iranian and
Saudi officials announced that the two countries would soon
sign a security pact.[7] 'Abdallah also has demonstrated less of
a willingness to follow U.S. policy on Iraq—a previous Saudi
tendency that has been a sore point with the radical Sunni
fundamentalists. The radical fundamentalists overseas seem
to be waiting to see what the crown prince will accomplish;
the secular opposition Committee Against Corruption in
Saudi Arabia (CACSA) issued a statement in 1999 that it will
give him a chance and not criticize him, and then it shut down
its web site.[8]

A Balance between the Modern and the Religious

Is it possible that 'Abdallah will restore "Faysal's order," a balance between modernization and tradition, while projecting
the image of a pious and uncorrupt king? Possibly. On the
modernization side, 'Abdallah has introduced the Internet
into Saudi Arabia (although this is heavily controlled via a
proxy server at the King 'Abd al-'Aziz City for Science and
Technology). 'Abdallah's people may have been behind a
rumor, or trial balloon, that spread in late 1998 that the kingdom was considering permitting women to drive. Pragmatism
lay behind the idea: It would end the need for nearly a half-
million foreign chauffeurs.[9] In 1999, 'Abdallah purposefully
sparked debates on two other controversial issues: incoming
tourism and expanded rights for women. International tour-

ism, which had for all intents and purposes been forbidden in the kingdom, was feared by conservatives as a "source of depravation and insecurity."[10] 'Abdallah followed up later that year by permitting some closely organized tourism, notably by the Smithsonian Institution in the United States.[11] The crown prince's April 1999 speech in the Eastern Province, in which he specifically addressed the need to involve women in "national participation,"[12] led to many articles in the Saudi press debating the merits of more female participation in public aspects of Saudi society.[13] 'Abdallah has also stepped out in public and strolled through a shopping center, an act that surprised many but seemed calculated to point up the difference between him and the ailing Fahd, and to make the crown prince seem more approachable.[14]

As for tradition, as the country celebrated its centenary in January 1999, Crown Prince 'Abdallah let the religious establishment flex its muscles. General Mufti Shaykh 'Abd al-'Aziz bin Baz condemned the celebrations as *bid'a* (innovation)—in general, Wahhabi Islam does not allow commemorations, even of the prophet's birthday. While not canceling the celebrations, the government did take heed by ordering decorations and colored lights removed from shops.[15] Moreover, 'Abdallah seems to be indicating that, as he moves closer to becoming king, he wishes to turn over a new leaf regarding the opposition. In 1997, he released one of the founders of the CDLR, Hamid Ibrahim al-Sulayfih, a move that may have signaled 'Abdallah's desire to put the problem of the radical Sunni fundamentalist opposition behind him.[16] In January 1998, 'Abdallah felt confident enough to release another CDLR founder, Shaykh Sulayman al-Rushudi.[17] Finally, in June 1999, 'Abdallah released the Awakening Shaykhs, Safar bin 'Abd al-Rahman al-Hawali and Salman bin Fahd al-'Awda, after nearly five years in captivity.[18] Releasing the shaykhs was a prudent, balanced step, following the opening of the debate on women and tourism. The terms of the shaykhs' release are unknown; in the past, the two shaykhs rejected offers of freedom on the condition that they stop their *da'wa* (proselytizing) activities. 'Abdallah does indeed seem to be attempting to reach a balance between competing forces. Whether his achievements will match those of King Faysal bin 'Abd al-'Aziz, only time will tell.

Islamic legitimacy is central to the rule of the Al Sa'ud; the regime will do everything necessary to confront anyone who tries to undermine that aspect. If Crown Prince 'Abdallah is successful in finding a balance that placates the radical fundamentalists, then the Saudi royal family will be in good shape for many years. When 'Abdallah finally becomes king, he will have to appoint a crown prince. This occasion may become tense, particularly if, in the struggle for the title of crown prince, an appeal is made to Islamic legitimacy by certain claimants allying with radicals. Another issue that warrants monitoring is the state of the armed forces, particularly the tribally based SANG. So far, there has been no destabilizing influence in the armed forces, but there are indications that matters are not entirely under control there. Although the extent of radical Sunni fundamentalist sympathizers in the Saudi armed forces is difficult to assess, in August 1996, a "U.S. source with close connections to the Saudi military" said Lt. Gen. Ahmad bin Ibrahim Bihayri, the commander of the Saudi Air Force, had been held accountable, among other misdeeds, for the activities of a group of radical fundamentalist officers who had been holding meetings. According to the source, Bihayri was fired on April 9, 1996.[19] The incident somehow merited little mention in the press.

Increasing Awareness of Social Discontent

Social discontent does not always breed radical Islamic fundamentalism, but it can certainly be a contributing factor. Most Saudis care little about politics, but they would be delighted if the princes could restrain some of their more overt signs of corruption, favoritism, and nepotism. A little is fine, even expected, but the appearance of propriety would be welcome. It will be interesting to observe the behavior of the recently released Awakening Shaykhs. Will they criticize the Al Sa'ud's foreign policy and the implementation of the *shari'a* (Islamic law)? Perhaps they now have the ear of the government and will be able to convey their views in a direct but private manner.

The modern Saudi state, since its founding by 'Abd al-'Aziz (Ibn Sa'ud) in 1902, has always been able to handle domestic political challenges. Indeed, the royal family has handled its opposition quite well. An Islamic revolution is unlikely—Saudis prefer stability to an uncertain future—so matters would have to worsen much more than they already have. The Al Sa'ud has links to all the most important tribes and elites, and its security services can usually nip problems in the bud. It is quite adept at exploiting the weakness of the opposition, and prefers accommodation to confrontation. "There are no permanent enemies here in Saudi Arabia," said Prince Sultan bin Salman, the son of the governor of Riyadh.[20] Indeed, the Saudi opposition seems at the time of this writing to be in a state of suspended animation.

But even such times as these are not entirely without opposition activity. During 2000, the opposition's use of the Internet has picked up again, and several opposition sites have emerged, demonstrating that while matters may be mostly quiet inside, the opposition voice is still clamoring to be heard.[21] Perhaps more seriously, in early August a gunman opened fire at a compound housing British and U.S. personnel in Khamis Mushayt, 'Asir Province. The attack left one Saudi policeman dead and two others injured. The Saudi would say only that that he was "a student."[22]

For foreigners concerned with the future of the kingdom, the lesson of the radical fundamentalist movement in Saudi Arabia is that closer attention must be paid to religious trends within and outside the religious establishment. A hidden struggle continues regarding who will determine the da'wa of Bin 'Abd Al-Wahhab. One must read for oneself what dissidents write and listen to their taped talks. Although the subject matter is sometimes difficult for foreigners, the Saudi royal family and westernized liberal Saudis are not always the best interpreters of this material. Saudi countermeasures are also worthy of attention. The Al Sa'ud is not quick to acknowledge dissent, but the increase of discord in Islamic institutions, particularly those concerning da'wa, is a signal that the leadership is worried.

Notes

1. Even after Bin Baz's death in 1999, the former top cleric's writing and persona are still being used by the government in this legitimizing manner. See the government's Bin Baz website at http://www.binbaz.org.sa.

2. U.S. Energy Information Administration, *Country Brief: Saudi Arabia*, February 1999, located online at www.eia.doe.gov/emeu/cabs/saudfull.html; International Monetary Fund (IMF) *International Financial Statistics, August 2000* (Washington: IMF, 2000); U.S. Bureau of the Census, International Data Base, located online at www.census.gov/ipc/www/idbnew.html; Douglas Jehl, "For Ordinary Saudis, Days of Oil and Roses Are Over," *New York Times*, March 20, 1999, p. A1; Agence France-Presse, September 4, 2000.

3. Joshua Teitelbaum, "Saudi Arabia," in Ami Ayalon and Bruce Maddy-Weitzman, eds., *Middle East Contemporary Survey (MECS) 1994* (Boulder, Colo.: Westview, 1996), pp. 548–582; Joshua Teitelbaum, "Saudi Arabia," in Bruce Maddy-Weitzman, ed., *MECS 1995* (Boulder, Colo.: Westview, 1997), pp. 532–561.

4. Nawaf Obaid and Patrick Clawson, "The 1999 Saudi Budget: Reforms in the Face of Acute Problems," Washington Institute for Near East Policy, *PolicyWatch*, no. 359, January 5, 1999; U.S. Energy Information Administration (EIA), *Country Brief: Saudi Arabia*, February 1999, online at http://www.eia.doe.gov/emeu/cabs/saudfull.html.

5. EIA, *Country Brief: Saudi Arabia*, February 1999; Simon Henderson, "Crucial Tests Await New Saudi Oil Council," The Washington Institute for Near East Policy, *PolicyWatch*, no. 435, January 24, 2000; "Supreme Intentions," *Gulf Business* 4, no. 6 (October 1999), online at http://www.gulfbusiness.com. For a recent, in-depth study of these bodies and oil politics in the kingdom, see Nawaf Obaid, *The Oil Kingdom at 100: Petroleum Policymaking in Saudi Arabia* (Washington: The Washington Institute for Near East Policy, 2000).

6. Radio Riyadh, December 8, 1998, in "United Kingdom : Saudi Crown Prince's Remarks to GCC Meeting Weighed," Foreign Broadcast Information Service Near East and South Asia daily report (online), FBIS-NES-93-343, December 8, 1998.

7. *Mideast Mirror*, May 19, 1999; Radio Riyadh, May 23, 1999, in "Iranian

Aide Cited on Relations with U.S., Regional Topics," FBIS-NES-99-0525 (online), May 25, 1995; Reuters, July 4, 7, 2000.

8. Formerly at http://www.saudhouse.com.

9. Agence France-Presse, November 1, 1998.

10. Agence France-Presse, April 7, 1999 (quoting Prof. Ahmad Turkistani, Imam Muhammad bin Sa'ud Islamic University in Riyadh).

11. Smithsonian Institution travel brochure, "Inside Saudi Arabia." In April 2000, the kingdom established a tourism agency, headed by the minister of defense, Sultan bin 'Abd al-'Aziz. Agence France-Presse, May 8, 2000.

12. See *al-Riyad*, April 13, 1999.

13. See *al-'Ukaz*, April 20, 1999; *al-Yawm*, May 28, 1999.

14. Howard Schneider, "Saudi Arabia Finds Calm after Storm," *Washington Post*, January 9, 2000, p. A1.

15. Agence France-Presse, January 4, 1999; Reuters, January 4, 1999; *Times* (London), January 5, 1999. Shaykh Bin Baz died in mid-May 1999, replaced by the deputy General Mufti, Shaykh 'Abd Al-'Aziz bin 'Abdallah Al Al-Shaykh. Reuters, May 13, 1999; Associated Press, May 15, 1999.

16. See *al-Quds al-'Arabi*, April 15, 1997; Liberty for the Muslim World, communiqué, April 14, in MSANEWS, April 15, 1997.

17. See *al-Quds al-'Arabi*, January 7, 1998; *al-Quds al-'Arabi*, February 25, 1998; *al-Quds al-'Arabi*, July 27, 1998.

18. See *al-Quds al-'Arabi*, June 25, 1998.

19. Edward Cody, "Saudi Islamic Radicals Target U.S., Royal Family," *Washington Post*, August 15, 1996, p. A1; *Jane's Defence Weekly*, October 9, 1996.

20. Howard Schneider, "Saudi Arabia Finds Calm After a Storm," *Washington Post*, January 9, 2000, p. A1.

21. See, for example, the Sunni site, http://www.salman-safar.org, and the Shi'i site, http://www.alharmain.org.

22. *Mideast Mirror*, August 9, 2000; Agence France-Presse, August 9, 10, 2000.